A Life in the News

A LIFE IN THE NEWS

Tony Parsons

HARBOUR PUBLISHING

1 2 3 4 5 — 13 12 11 10 09

Harbour Publishing Co. Ltd.
P.O. Box 219, Madeira Park, BC, V0N 2H0
www.harbourpublishing.com

Cover photograph by Jeff Vinnick
All photographs courtesy Tony Parsons unless otherwise noted
Edited by Betty Keller
Printed and bound in Canada

Harbour Publishing acknowledges financial support from the Government of Canada through the Book Publishing Industry Development Program and the Canada Council for the Arts, and from the Province of British Columbia through the BC Arts Council and the Book Publishing Tax Credit.

Library and Archives Canada Cataloguing in Publication

Parsons, Tony, 1939–
  A life in the news / by Tony Parsons.

ISBN 978-1-55017-461-8

  1. Parsons, Tony, 1939–. 2. Television news anchors—British Columbia—Biography. 3. Television news anchors—Ontario—Biography.
I. Title.

PN4913.P373A3 2009   070.43092   C2009-904813-2

For Tammy,
with love and gratitude

Contents

The Parsonage Family of England

My FIRST EXPOSURE TO BROADCASTING was as a child in England listening to the daily dramas and comedy shows on BBC Radio. We were fans of *Dick Barton, Special Agent*, and *PC 49*, and comedians Arthur Askey and George Formby. Our family received a regular BBC bulletin called *Radio Times*, and I remember seeing photographs in it of announcers decked out in tuxedos to deliver the news, but I don't think anyone my age was impressed, much less inspired to set out to be a news anchor. In fact, that phrase wasn't even invented until 1952 when Walter Cronkite "anchored" the team of CBS reporters that worked the floor of the Republican and Democratic political conventions. Besides, my friends and I were all offspring of labour-minded mothers and fathers, labour in this case meaning not the political party, but the use of your hands to make a living.

Although by trade my father was a carpenter, by the late 1930s he had become a London policeman. Then in the spring of 1939 when the Second World War loomed and the Royal Air Force started taking recruits, he signed up and was posted to Gosport on the south coast of England, a town that was home to an RAF flight training school as well as headquarters for Coastal Forces Command. The family followed him there, and that is how I came to be born in Gosport on June 29, 1939, the fourth child of John and Julie Parsonage. I was christened Anthony (to honour my mother's only brother) Joseph.

Unfortunately, because of Gosport's military importance, the town became one of the first targets of German air raids in the fall and winter of 1939–40. London, on the other hand, had yet to be targeted for concentrated bombing, so my mother packed up the family—my older brother, John, my two older sisters, Anne and Phyllis, and myself—and moved us back to the west London district of Ealing. My mother's parents and siblings lived nearby in the suburb of White City. Her father had come from Italy before World War I to join other relatives who owned a gelato business in the west end of London, and it was there that his five daughters and one son (my mother was the second youngest of his family) had all been born.

Although my family's move back to London in the winter of 1939–40 mattered very little to me as I was just a baby, living in London during the next few years meant that air-raid sirens, search lights and the drone of planes became pretty much the sights and sounds of my early childhood. As I grew a little older, I recall that some of our fun times were spent in the streets picking up bomb fragments after a German raid, but it must have been a terrifying time for my mother, especially after London became a target for V-1 rockets in the summer of 1944. As a result, when the government once again ordered the evacuation of women and children, she must have been happy to take us to the picturesque seaside town of Appledore in Devon. To our little family, shielded from the daily prospect of handling the terrors of war, the small town seemed idyllic. Just the name was enough to calm us all down, and it remained that way until the day a buzz bomb crashed into the block of flats where my mother's parents lived in White City; the bodies of my grandmother and two of my mother's sisters were later found in the rubble. Not long afterward, my grandfather also died, grief having simply overtaken him.

When our mother left us in Appledore to go up to London for the family funerals, the woman who was to look after us while she was away suddenly took on the image of the worst kind of Dickensian villain, all malice and not a whit of sympathy or understanding. My brother and sisters went into rebel mode, between them hatching a plot to escape. Ten-year-old John, being the eldest, was the ringleader, my sisters went along with it, and I, just five years old and not really understanding what it was all about, became a willing conspirator. Somehow we managed a raid on the monster's pantry, making off with some bread, a jar of jam, a few rashers of bacon and some eggs. Added to that was a small frying pan and some matches. The plan was to head off into the countryside, set up camp in some farmer's field and hunker down until our mother's return.

But we underestimated the enemy. Minutes after we had established a hideout in a wide, dry ditch behind a hedgerow in the corner of a field and began to cook our stolen meal over a fire of sticks and leaves, there she was, looming over us like an avenging angel. I swear there were flames shooting out of her nostrils. We surrendered. She herded four whimpering kids across the field, down the narrow road to town and committed us to captivity once again. We never tried anything like it again, especially after she told my mother and we got a second dressing-down.

We left Appledore soon after this event, and life as a family began again in an enormous, four-storey house on Kirchen Road in Ealing. I recall the top part of the house was rented out to an Irish family. This was the house to which my father returned after being "demobbed" from the RAF in 1947. For most of the war years, he had commanded a torpedo boat for Air-Sea Rescue, collecting downed flyers from the English Channel. I hadn't seen much of him during those years, and after May 1945 when the war in Europe ended, he had been posted to the Iraqi city of Basra in some sort of peacekeeping role. Occasionally he had come home on leave, and sometimes he would take one or other of us on a trip into London to see a movie or have lunch at the Lyons Teahouse, but it was never a pleasant experience as we were deathly afraid of speaking out of turn or saying something he might take offence to. On the whole he seemed uninterested in us and anxious to get back to Basra to be with his cronies. He was a sombre disciplinarian, and it was only much later that I figured out that he used his uniform as a badge of authority to set himself apart from others. Earlier in life he had worn one as a copper on the London city police force, then as a flight lieutenant in the air force, later as a prison guard in Guelph, Ontario, and in his final job as a customs inspector on the Blue Water Bridge between Sarnia, Ontario, and Port Huron, Michigan. It was his licence, it seemed, to lord it over everyone, including his wife and children. In addition, he was well over six feet tall and that just added to the image he tried to create.

My mother, on the other hand, throughout all the hardship of her life, was as close to sainthood as any person can get. She was a tiny woman with a beatific face who lived her life for everyone around her, starting, of course, with her kids. We didn't exactly grow up poor in London, but there were lots of things we would have liked to have had that were beyond the family's reach. That said, if it had not been for Mother, the things that kept us safe and comfortable would have been unattainable. Despite the lack of money during the war years while my father was doing service, she always seemed to be able to cope, providing the necessities by budgeting the little that my father sent her from his air-force pay packet. Later, in Canada when there was no financial support forthcoming from my father, she always found a job. She was a store clerk at Woolworth's for a time. She took on cleaning jobs for neighbours and sometimes offered her services as a babysitter. In the late fifties in Kitchener, Ontario, she worked at a dairy just around the corner from our house, scooping ice cream out of huge buckets into cones for kiddie clients. And she got me involved in that one by persuading the manager to hire me on weekends to lug those tubs of ice cream up a flight of stairs from a huge basement freezer room. It was hard work even when the cold storage area offered relief on the hottest days of an Ontario summer.

Mother always managed to find a way to replace our worn-out or outgrown clothing, and I remember—perhaps more from family photos of the day rather than actual recall—that my sisters were always dressed neatly and none of us ever looked as if we were going without when it came to clothes or food. In fact, there was never a lack of food on our table during or after the war in England or after we moved to Canada, even if it was just "bubble and squeak," that fried-up combination of yesterday's mashed potatoes and cabbage, so named because, as it cooked, it would actually bubble and squeak. She served other things as well that wouldn't meet the standards of today's healthy diets. Some days, usually after Sunday's roast beef dinners, we were treated to "toast and drippings"—the juice from the roast and the fat that had congealed over it spread on slices of toasted bread. "Toad in the Hole"—sausage cooked in a Yorkshire pudding batter—was another favourite. It could be that the diet that fuelled us in those days is the reason none of us can think of a thing in our adult lives that we won't eat or, at the very least, try.

I am not implying by the foregoing that my mother was a cook, good or otherwise, though you would think that with her Italian background she would be a whiz among the pots and pans. Alas, she never was. My father, perhaps in self-defence, did most of the cooking during his infrequent stays with us. His greatest mishap occurred one Christmas while we were living in Feversham when he somehow laced the turkey stuffing with curry powder thinking, he said later, that it was sage. But my mother was the author of disaster after disaster. Her idea of sauce for her over-cooked pasta was a goo of tomato paste and canned whole tomatoes simmered in a frying pan and finished off with handfuls of grated cheddar cheese. It was ghastly—rather like eating a fistful of rubber bands. But her lack of culinary talent never seemed to bother her. Later in life her staples included never-ending pots of tea with biscuits or toast lathered in butter and a box of Peek Frean cookies. She also doted on English crumpets, those round, rubbery things with holes throughout, which always left a trail of melted butter between the toaster in her kitchen and her dining table.

But if she had no talent for cooking, Mother could sure write letters, certainly in terms of volume. For her it was a lifelong habit, and I can remember running to the local post-office box at least a couple of times a week with sometimes a dozen letters clutched in my hand. Over her eighty-plus years I don't think she ever lost touch with anyone who crossed her path.

In my mother's house you would not dare say a word against the royal family. Of course, in the war years the royals were beyond criticism anyway, their lives untarnished by gossip or internecine problems. They were the guiding lights who, along with Winston Churchill, made those years tolerable for my mother and others like her. In fact, she was so enamoured of kings and queens that, whenever there was a public appearance by the monarch, wherever there was a parade, you could spot my mother behind the metal barricades craning her neck for a look at them as they waved—I'm sure she thought to her alone—on their way to and from Buckingham Palace.

She carried her royalist fervour to Canada when we came here in 1948 by reading the British newspapers sent to her by her sisters and twisting the dials on our console radio to find whatever she could in the way of "royal news." What she never did, however, was try to draw her children into that worshipful state—for which I am thankful. I look at the day-to-day lives of the current royals (I always buy a copy of the *Sunday Times* and the *Mail on Sunday*) and I wonder what my mother would think of those people now. I also wonder what she ever saw in them in the first place.

More than the royals, though, my mother loved her family, her kids and her siblings. (Her brother and two sisters survived the war.) She kept us kids together after she and my father had decided, without actually announcing it, that they would be better off living apart. Not a divorce, mind you. My Catholic mother would never even think of that. During their years of separation it was not unusual for my father to tote his dirty laundry to my mother's house or apartment and come back later to pick up a load of freshly washed and neatly ironed shirts, clean socks and underwear. Given my father's track record as a husband and father I found that, in retrospect, pretty amazing.

For my brother and my sisters she was a rock, but she ran a tight ship. She had rules about curfews as most parents do but, even though there might be a finger-wagging warning if we were late, her anger was short-lived. The only time I ever saw her fly into a rage was one night in Feversham when my brother arrived home late at night and tried to sneak up to the room he shared with me to avoid a confrontation with Mom. She was ready for him. Every rural home in that area had a .22 calibre rifle, and the one in our house was used by my brother John to hunt squirrels or some other helpless species. That night it ended up in the hands of my irate mother who was beside herself over his behaviour and his lack of remorse at overshooting his curfew. I'm not sure there was even any ammunition in the thing, but I do remember hiding in the corner of the room, violently shaking and afraid that the weapon would suddenly go off in her hands and rob me of the only brother I ever had. I think John got the message and Mother backed off, having made her point in a most forceful way. And it wasn't something I ever saw again. (When Mother and I were both much older, we sat one evening sipping brandy and I reminded her of the incident. She just laughed and nodded.)

It seems to me now, looking back, that given the times and the circumstances, we were a fairly typical family. In the first place, all of us but Kathy, my youngest sister who was born in Canada, were born British, which in itself presents some built-in characteristics, stoicism among them. We were typically "stiff upper lip," all of us, though more, of course, because of my father's influence than my mother's who, due to her Italian heritage, put her heart and soul into raising her family and wore that heart on her sleeve. The girls inherited her ways. I didn't.

The Parsonage Family
Moves to Canada

I GUESS PEACETIME BRITAIN didn't suit my father. Shortly after he returned home for good, he began making plans to take us all to another part of the world. First he thought Iraq had something to offer, then it was Australia and finally, because my mother had a friend living in Canada who would sponsor us as immigrants, he decided to move us all to the Georgian Bay area of Ontario. For the five of us kids (my sister Diane had recently been born) it was a staggering decision. Goodbye to friends and family and hello to a new world that none of us knew anything about. Our sense of adventure simply wasn't up for it.

My sisters were doing well in school, and my fourteen-year-old brother had his first real girlfriend. I had established myself as a fairly competent student at St. Joseph's

Catholic School, managing to cope with the ferocious discipline of the nuns who ran the establishment, one of whom always brandished a willow stick. And she used it often. One whack across the palm of your hand or the back of your legs and you were soon back in line. I had joined the local Cub Scout group, earned a few easy badges, and had even gone on a field trip or two. One was a trip to Ireland that featured a rough (beyond belief) ferry trip and a few rainy nights in a leaky tent. The weather became so miserable, I remember, that we had to transfer to a local farmer's barn for the duration.

But in October 1948 Father uprooted us all. It turned out to be an auspicious departure. I don't know how the London newspapers got wind of it, but we were news in several editions of the infamous tabloids and even the *Toronto Star* because we were apparently the largest family ever to immigrate to Canada via a scheduled airline, Trans Canada, later Air Canada. Thus, our brief moment of fame. I'm not sure if it made up for what lay ahead. I know that it wasn't any compensation for my mother. She was later to confide that Canada was her idea of the ends of the earth, and she cried most of the way there and for months after we arrived.

Getting there was definitely not half the fun because our trip was by no means a non-stop, direct flight. The plane had to put down in the Azores Islands and we spent the night there in military barracks while a storm front passed and we refuelled. The following day we went on to St John's, Newfoundland, and then Goose Bay, Labrador, where we climbed down the steps to the frozen, snowbound tarmac to stretch our legs for a few minutes. We stopped again in Montreal and eventually arrived in Toronto, more than twenty-four hours after we left London.

We were billeted for the night at a Salvation Army shelter to wait for our train, which left the next morning for our final destination, the town of Feversham. That Sally Ann stay introduced me to bananas, which had been unavailable in England during the war, and to Chiclets chewing gum, something else I had never seen.

The train trip was uneventful but long and tiring, and it took us only as far as Flesherton, the nearest large town to Feversham. For the rest of the journey we had to pile into the back of the very small van that usually delivered the rural mail and groceries throughout the snowbelt that cut into Grey County. And we soon found out what snowbelt meant because, although it was only October, the road to Feversham was already flanked by eight-foot snowdrifts. Even for our experienced driver, Laurie Sewell, the road was slippery and treacherous and he admitted to more than a few anxious moments.

Feversham was desolate and cold. The village consisted of a couple of dozen houses and two general stores, one of which doubled as a gas station. There was a bank, a public school and a couple of churches, neither representing the religion my mother was clinging to. To get to a Roman Catholic church, the local believers banded together to drive for more than an hour along rough country roads, but even with this inconvenience I think my mother missed Mass on only a few Sundays.

My father must have hated the town on sight because

he was gone within a few weeks, taking a job with Ontario Hydro near Barrie where the company was building a huge substation to serve an increasing number of customers. It was months before we saw him again. He left us in a rented upper-floor flat on a farm just outside the village. It was owned by a rough-and-tumble guy named Tom Stephens and his wife Naomi, who would for a while become my mother's confidante and friend. Naomi was sympathetic and concerned that my mother had been left to cope with five kids on her own in unfamiliar and, to my mother, unfriendly circumstances. Naomi, who had two small kids of her own, was never far away when my mother needed help and encouragement. And that was often.

As little money was coming from my father, Mother was forced to establish a line of credit at the general store owned by John Robinson, the local equivalent of the "richest man in town." Stout and mustachioed, he was clearly living the good life, though he was beginning to feel the competition from the other store run by Herb and Madge Eby. So John had to come up with a marketing ploy that might give him back the upper hand. For every dollar his customers spent in his store, he decreed that they would receive a piece of china, and eventually if they spent enough, they could accumulate full sets, eight settings I guess, and thereby he might have invented "value-added consumerism."

Sooner or later my father came home. It was a pleasant break for my mother, and even though we had resented his absence over the months, we were happy to have him back. He would soon be gone again, but before he left, he had to settle the bills my mother had run up at Robinson's General

Store. John in his generosity had given my mother full rein on credit, and her unpaid account was huge. Fortunately, my father had come back with the wherewithal to make things right, and that's when John's customer appreciation plan kicked in for us. We went home with enough china–ware that day to set up a medium-sized hotel. We definitely had no use for that many plates, cups and saucers, and it might, right now, be sitting in its original cardboard boxes in the derelict building that once was Tom Stephens' barn.

In time our lives in Feversham became bearable. We all found friends and spent time together rafting on the Beaver River, fishing for trout, working summers on local farms, stealing corn, learning how to smoke, reading voraciously, and just growing up. Of course, the winters there seemed to last forever. The middle of April would often feature a snowstorm that covered the neighbouring fields and hills, so the only thing to do was relax and enjoy it. As the near-est ski hill was miles away on treacherous roads, we created our own on rolling terrain that was more suited to cross-country than downhill skiing. We carved out a few tobog-gan runs that provided about ten seconds of thrill or we went sledding on the only road through town when traffic had moved on—traffic being the occasional horse-drawn sleigh that the farmers used to pick up feed and supplies in the months when their trucks and cars were locked away for the season in the garage or the barn. But the really big deal was an impromptu game of shinny on the nearest frozen pond—my introduction to the Canadian game of hockey.

Of course, no British schoolboy ever grows up yearn-ing to play ice hockey. More likely they dream about soccer fields or cricket patches or Formula One motor racing or maybe even field hockey but never a game played in freezing conditions and featuring sticks and pucks. Not that the game is never played in England. There are small regional teams, and an effort was once made to introduce the game on a larger scale, but it never became a part of British sporting life. That's why it was so new to me when we arrived in Canada. To say that I was bad at it would be an understatement. I was an embarrassment to the national pastime and pretty much stayed that way, even though I did learn to skate on those bumpy pond surfaces and the much smoother ice at the local rink.

Every small town in the area had a rink. It was usually adjacent to the baseball field or some other summer sports facility. Ours was in a riverside park in a building that was more of a barn than an arena, and the wind whistled between the planks of its wooden walls. You dared not skate without a parka, one of those with fur around the hood (in those days the anti-fur lobby didn't exist), and warm gloves. The rink's other life was as the main centre for our Fall Fair, a part of country living that still endures. But on Saturday nights in winter there was music to skate to, played by what passed as a disc jockey, and it attracted young people from across the area. Many a romance began on those nights in the Feversham rink. Round and round everyone went, ducking into the co-ed dressing room every once in a while to warm up with a cup of steaming hot cocoa, then inviting some member of the opposite sex to take a turn around the rink. This required holding hands and could foster thoughts of bigger and better dates to come. My brother, John, was right in there. He was tall, as was my father, and very handsome and was more the pursued than the pursuer.

There were no leagues as such, but from time to time there were hockey games featuring some of the older, accomplished players, some of whom could actually skate backward, which, I thought, was the ultimate skill. These guys just played the game for the love of it and, from my perspective, played it well at that level. After my own very basic skills began to develop, I was invited to become a member of a new peewee team, the level that exists at the very bottom of the hockey food chain and mostly features players who skate on their ankles. I suspect that they included me simply because I was another warm body and they were in desperate need of players. I didn't last long. After a few frigid pre-sunrise Saturday mornings of being bussed with the others to nearby Flesherton, a town much bigger than ours with a regulation-sized rink, I was taken aside and firmly told that I was being uninvited—or in today's major-league parlance, put on waivers. Nobody else would have me, though, and thus ended my hockey career—at least the playing aspect.

Hockey, by the way, was my mother's passion. Or should I say she was passionate about the Toronto Maple Leafs? As far as we know, she had never been a sports fan of any stripe during her days in the UK, and like most immigrants of that era she probably didn't know the game existed until she got here, but she took to it immediately. She loved the likes of Turk Broda, the Leafs' goalie, and all the great Toronto players of his era, and she followed the team's fortunes every step of the way. She adopted the fan's disdainful attitude toward any referee who called a penalty against her beloved side, and she adored any member of her adopted team who excelled on *Hockey Night in Canada* in those days before expansion. We, her children, never understood her fascination for the game, given her Anglo-Italian background, and she never explained.

It was shortly after my brief hockey career ended that my growing up was interrupted by a bout of rheumatic fever. It was May 1951 and I was eleven years old. It was a long and debilitating experience, first in a hospital in Markham, the nearest town to have full-fledged health facilities. Then, because my condition worsened and the doctors feared it might escalate to rheumatoid arthritis, I was moved to the much larger and more advanced Hospital for Sick Children in Toronto. I was left there for twelve weeks to recover, sucking back handfuls of aspirin and digesting sulpha drugs every day. That was a lonely time for me as I watched other parents show up on a regular basis to see how their stricken children were getting along. My mother had no car, Toronto was a long way from Feversham, and my brother and sisters needed her attention. By that time my father had left Feversham again, though to give him his due, I have to say that he did show up once, bringing my brother to see me. It was outside visiting hours but he managed to persuade a sleepy nurse to let them into my ward, visit for a few minutes and quickly go. As I recall, that was my only visit from anyone in the family. I did have other visitors, elderly volunteers who seemed to be trying to make their lives useful in their advancing years. I did appreciate them, especially one guy who came every week dressed in cowboy garb right down to his shiny alligator boots. He called himself "Texas Cyclone Westerwelt." I don't remember receiving any formal schooling while I was in hospital, but there was lots of reading and doing puzzles to pass the time. There were complications after I came home; I remember still being on drugs and they wouldn't let me walk very far, and a year later I had a recurrence of the disease. However, I survived that easily and today have few if any effects.

There was, by the way, no impact on the family budget because of my illness as there was a research project underway at the hospital at the time, and the doctors had asked that I be included in the program as a sort of guinea pig. Researchers were trying to determine if the disease promoted heart problems. I never heard the results of their work, but because of that research project, what could have been a very expensive stay in the hospital became a free ride, so to speak.

By the time I was well again, the family had moved to Kitchener, Ontario, and I was enrolled there in grade nine at St. Jerome's College—really a Catholic high school that catered to both day students and boarders. Gary Cowan, who went on to be an amateur golf champion, was one of my classmates there (though none of his talent rubbed off on me.) The school was run by the Jesuit order of priests and brothers, who were stern but ruled in good humour, and under their guidance I began to form ideas about my "purpose in life." My mother would have loved to have seen me enter the priesthood as she would have scored big brownie points with God, but there was no way I would go in that direction. I thought law might be an option—in the Perry Mason style—but while I was still making my decision, my parents packed us up again and we landed in Sarnia, the so-called Chemical Valley, home to oil-refining plants run by Shell, Esso, Polymer and the like. If you went to high school in Sarnia, it was almost taken for granted that you would end up working shifts in one of those plants after graduation and for the best part of the rest of your life. But after I worked one summer in a factory that produced fibreglass insulation materials that left me scratching my skin raw, I was determined never to succumb to that life.

I was confident that there were better days ahead. And, as it turned out, I was right. My real interest lay in English composition, literature and history, but because I was stunned by subjects like trigonometry and Latin, I opted for the vocational stream. My course load was, therefore, heavy on the practical things in life, such as auto mechanics, mechanical drafting, woodworking and sheet metal fabrication, as I was actually hoping that I could slide through high school on the basis of mechanical attributes and skills my father never thought I had.

He excelled at carpentry and all related skills. He could hang wallpaper almost with his eyes closed. He could certainly qualify as a house painter as he did that with hardly any effort at all. In later years I saw him cobble together custom-made aluminum storm windows in a small, cement-block building on the outskirts of Sarnia. He even taught night-school mathematics when he couldn't find something manual that would supply a paycheque—which reminds me of the first night he brought home money he'd earned teaching. They paid cash in those days, and he strutted into the kitchen at just about suppertime and with a great flourish threw a handful of banknotes into the air. As they fluttered to the floor, he was laughing, something he didn't do very often, and it was evident that he had spent a bit of what he'd earned at the local Legion or a favourite bar on his way home. It was a happy moment in a household that didn't see that many as drink would eventually be my father's downfall. I never told him then or later how he amazed me, how everything he put his hand to he did so well. And in later years he never mentioned to me how proud he was that I achieved some success in my career. He did tell others, though, and I heard it from them.

But back when I was in high school, I was still trying to convince myself that he was wrong about my lack of trades-man's skills. My big opportunity came when I was given an assignment in woodworking class to build a coffee table. It was supposed to be round and polished. I got the round part right but the table rocked—though not in today's ver-nacular. It literally rocked back and forth because each of its four legs was a different length. I took it home and, without showing it to anyone, tossed it in the rubbish pile in the garage. We didn't own a car so whatever room my table took up didn't matter.

Fortunately, in those days our school offered weekly classes in occupational guidance that were designed to point us in the direction of a career. And it was in one of those classes that the seed was planted that led to my more than half a century as a broadcaster. Our "occupational guide" in those classes, the man who was supposed to steer us toward a career that included a paycheque, was the same man who taught us history, where we were tested regularly on our ability to stand in front of the rest of the class and read aloud from whatever chapter he had chosen. On one of the days when I became the designated reader, he said to me afterward in front of all my classmates, "You know, Parsonage (that was still my surname then), you have a good voice and you read well. Perhaps you should think about getting into broadcasting." The idea took off. He did his part, getting information for me about a new Radio and Television Arts course at Ryerson Institute of Technology in Toronto. He later added to that a three-hundred-dollar scholastic grant from, believe it or not, the Imperial Order of the Daughters of the Empire. Their purpose may be lost in time and I'm not sure today what they stood for, but their cheque got me going, and I was accepted at Ryerson.

The Radio Years

THE RYERSON INSTITUTE OF TECHNOLOGY was a disaster for me, probably through no fault of the teachers. They had all had previous experience in the broadcasting industry before they landed there, though some of them did seem to bring the ring of truth to the old dictum "He who can, does. He who cannot, teaches." But the school was new as was the idea of preparing people for broadcasting careers. It was, in fact, a business that had only limited job opportunities until it expanded to include television. Unfortunately, I lacked the patience to stand in lineups waiting to test my skills on antiquated equipment passed down to us by local radio stations, stuff that probably would have been thrown onto the garbage pile if it hadn't been for us. And when I discovered that archery was part of the curriculum, I gave up altogether. From then on I spent more time in Steele's Bar around the corner on Yonge Street than I did in the classroom. (Like father, like son?) At seventeen I was under the legal drinking age, but there was always someone who, for the price of a beer, would lend me a driver's licence that said otherwise.

I left Ryerson before the end of my first year, deciding that experience in the field would push me ahead faster than classroom instruction at its best, and I went back home to Sarnia without the broadcasting job I coveted. It was after a month or so of anguish and menial work like cleaning beaten-up refrigerators and stoves in a store that sold used appliances that I hit on a plan that might at least get me in the door of some small station. I found a directory of stations in Ontario, chose the ones I thought might need an inexperienced but eager announcer, disc jockey, news reader or whatever and fired off letters that leaned heavily on my experience at Ryerson—not mentioning, of course, that I was a dropout. From a dozen applications I got two replies. One was from a station in Chatham. The manager wanted to know the name of my pastor, and whether I was a smoker because apparently that was forbidden in his operation. I was a smoker then and knew I couldn't quit even for the sake of a job. I didn't write back.

The other reply came from CJCS, a small station with studios in the Windsor Hotel in the little town of Stratford. It had started as an amateur station, 10AK, in 1928, but when Roy Thomson bought it six years later, he changed the call letters to CJCS and within a year bumped it up to 50 watts. A local lawyer, Frank M. Squires, bought it in 1942; a year later the station's power was increased to 100 watts and then to 250 watts in 1947, a signal that could still barely be heard on the outskirts of town. Squires also contracted with the CBC to become a Dominion Network affiliate and began broadcasting from seven in the morning until eleven at night (two hours less on Sundays). The Rogers Group's Countryside Holdings owned the station from March 1954, but Squires had bought it back just a couple of months before I applied there for a job in the spring of 1957. By then the station was managed by Stan Tapley with Bill Inkol as program and sports director and Bruce Schulthies as news director.

I took the bus from Sarnia one Saturday morning after Tapley invited me to come by for an interview. After a quick hello, he directed me to sit in and watch the shift announcer who was on air at the time. I was dumbstruck. These were the days when the announcer was expected to "announce-op," that is, he had to talk and operate the record turntables and audio-tape machines at the same time. This shift announcer, whose name I can't recall, was good at it, and as I watched him I never thought I could be. How could anyone ever do both those things at once and still think?

When the session ended, I left the station and went straight back to the bus depot, all ready to buy my return ticket to Sarnia there and then. I was just about to get back on the bus when it struck me what a coward I was. Why come all this way only to turn around and run away from my only job prospect? I went back to the station and found Tapley in his office. He hadn't even missed me. I would take the job, I told him, if he was still offering it. We agreed on a starting salary of twenty-four dollars a week, and I started two days later.

CJCS offered every service known to man. It catered to farmers, housewives, people who tuned in to find out who had died over the last couple of days, sports fans, listeners who wanted to get rid of things we'd find today in garage sales, and those in the "everyone else" category who actually wanted to hear the news. It was the perfect training situation for a beginning broadcaster, and it was encouraging to know that Lloyd Robertson had started his broadcasting career there just four years earlier (1952), though after a year he had moved on to CJOY in Guelph. In time I became the farm editor, women's editor, solemn reader of obituaries and hog prices and eventually the morning host from six to nine, playing music, giving weather reports and short news bulletins, and yes, managing to "announce-op" quite successfully. It was much the way Johnny Carson began on a similar radio station in Nebraska, but I'm sure he never made the mistakes that dogged me in those formative months.

One Sunday I had driven with friends to take in a jazz concert in Detroit. It was a long drive for one day, but we were all Dave Brubeck fans, and he didn't do many concerts we could get to. After the music and the euphoria of the concert we had to drive back to Stratford. It was the middle of the night when we got home, and I had to take the station to air the next morning. Okay, I thought, I can do this, but I was more tired than I knew and I fell asleep at the switch, so to speak. My head slumped over the control panel and I was jarred awake by the sound of the needle running on the last cut of an LP (a long-playing record)—kuh-puk, kuh-puk in the final groove—for how long I wasn't sure. This was bad enough, but my embarrassment was compounded by the fact that not one person called to complain. No one apparently noticed, not even the station manager.

Despite that, I soon came to enjoy my first job immensely and within two years I had upgraded my skills from none to a passable few. Then, even though I had made friends and had come to feel a sense of community in Stratford, I decided to return to Sarnia where my mother was still living with my youngest sister, who was proving to be quite a handful. My parents' marriage was long over by this time, though my father still showed up from time to time and later moved back to Sarnia to take a job as a customs inspector on the Blue Water Bridge. My mother was still finding jobs to keep the family fed and in school, but I figured I could help her out with monthly expenses by paying room and board. When I gave my notice at CJCS, I didn't expect Tapley to weep at the prospect of my departure from the station, but he told me that he couldn't care less about my leaving because it was his opinion that I would never make it in the business anyway.

I landed a job back home at CHOK in Sarnia, which proved to be a lateral move to say the least. That station, which had been launched in 1946, was a member of the CBC's Trans-Canada Network, so most of its programming originated in Toronto or Ottawa. I worked the late shift, four to midnight, and I was merely a disembodied voice, the one that intoned the station breaks in the style of James Earl Jones, "This is CHOK, Sarnia, Midway on the Seaway." Or something like that. The only sop to my ego was the eleven p.m. news package, a so-called "rip-and-read" effort, which meant you went to the teletype, literally ripped off the news items and read them verbatim on air.

Fortunately, the job in Sarnia was short-lived. Within a few months another station beckoned. Guelph was the home of the Ontario Agricultural College and not much else, but it did have a radio station, CJOY, that was heavily into rock and roll. I learned about a job opening for a DJ there from a trade magazine, and about the same time they heard about me from an acquaintance who worked there. I went to Guelph for an interview, and although I had very little experience in the direction CJOY was pointed, they took me on anyway. The program director, Don LeBlanc, spent the next couple of months trying but never convincing me that rock and roll was the way of the future. He was also determined to mould me into an energetic on-air personality. First he changed my name from Parsonage to Parsons because the shortened name was easier to say and easier for listeners to understand. It was a move that upset my father who thought that, if I was going to do this thing, I might at least keep the family name. But Parsons I became because the station had a policy of shortening things in keeping with their format. Their call letters became CeeJoy, and DJs had to call thermometers CeeJoy-mometers. I could never quite get my head or tongue around that one, and it would always come out CeeJoy-mom-eaters. At times LeBlanc complained that he didn't get the sense that I was happy and enthusiastic in my on-air presentations, and one day he took me into a studio, opened the only window onto the square below and told me to yell loud enough in a spirited CJOY announcer's manner that people would turn their heads and look up. Of course, I was embarrassed to do it because it's not my way, and consequently I did it so badly that not a soul looked up.

I was about two months into this struggle when along came Tom Darling, the general manager of CHML, a comparative broadcasting powerhouse in Hamilton, Ontario. He had come to Guelph to scout another member of the staff, a man much more experienced than I was at this point, but for some reason he preferred my style, and I packed my bags again and went down the highway.

The CHML Years

CHML HAD BEEN LAUNCHED back in September 1926 after the owner of Hamilton's first radio station, CKOC, pulled the plug on the broadcast of a sermon by a local minister who was expounding on Ontario's prohibition law. In response to this censorship, an ex-mayor of Hamilton, George Lees, headed up a new company called Maple Leaf Radio in order to secure a licence from the Radio Bureau in Ottawa. In its early years this tiny station, operating at just 50 watts, broadcast church services, pro-temperance speeches, bulletins from the police department, announcements of YMCA meetings, special programs for Mountain Sanatorium patients, hockey games and music. It also provided free airtime for charity fundraisers. But things began to change in 1936 when Ken Soble came to CHML as manager, and they changed more eight years later when he bought the station, mortgaging everything he owned to come up with the money. By this time the station's power had been ramped up to 5,000 watts, and it was on the air from six in the morning to one the following morning. In 1949 Soble built a new state-of-the-art facility for CHML at 848 Main Street in Hamilton, and that is where I went to work as a DJ in the spring of 1960. I was a couple of months short of my twenty-first birthday.

By that time CHML was a much more middle-of-the-road station than CJOY, and I thrived on the format, finally coming into my own as a minor radio personality. I began as a "floater," a substitute performer for no-shows or the sick, and worked with—or in the shadow of—some very talented people. Paul Reid, for instance, had a voice so incredibly modulated and deep that, when he was doing his show, his studio phone never stopped ringing. His charming persona seemed to float in the air, and his fans, understandably mostly women, always called craving a little personal attention. He didn't disappoint them. Another of those talented CHML people was Paul Hanover, who held down the coveted morning drive program for so long and so well that he earned the nickname "Mayor of the Morning." Perc Allen was our star sports commentator, rivalling Reid for popularity with our female audience. He had movie-star good looks and a smoking habit that eventually ended his life. Norm Marshall, who was also a legend in local radio, was the station's sports director as well as a sports commentator. While he doled out the sports scores, he chomped cigars into a repugnant mess, spraying the microphone with a dark brown mist. But he was one of the most affable men I've ever known. Gordie Tapp was also part of our lineup, doing a late night, thirty-minute program of music and corny jokes. He was the creator and voice of a leprechaun he called Barry Fitzperfect, who was a big hit with his fans. In 1969 Tapp left to become a founding member of the cast of the country-style TV show *Hee Haw* in the US.

I never achieved a permanent prime-time DJ spot at CHML and I even did all-nights for a while, so about three years into my eight-year stint there—which up till then was a record stay on a job for me—I changed directions. I had grown tired of being a DJ, of exploding what the management called "little bombs of happiness" every day. And I knew I wasn't really a good DJ. It was a way of working in the business but I realized it wasn't what I really wanted. It seemed to me that a newscaster's job would last longer than that of a DJ. I didn't want to be yesterday's DJ. Even with a limited knowledge about the actual gathering of news, I decided that my future might be in that area. Don Johnston, the news director, seemed a little excited about the idea when I put it to him. "Usually," he said, "it's the other way around—news people wanting to take on the glamour side of the business and becoming 'on-air personalities.'" So he consulted Tom Darling, and I was released from my duties as a "floater" and allowed a tryout in the newsroom.

I took to it quickly, learning to write accurately to hourly deadlines in readable style and eventually taking what I'd written to the studio to become a newscaster. I wasn't that good at first, but within a few months I was accepted by the pros in the news operation and, I guess, by the audience. Soon I was left to work alone on the four-to-midnight shift, writing through the evening, going out on stories between the major newscasts at six and eleven, reading the final show and then, before I left, preparing a batch of edited news bulletins for the overnight DJ.

Life at CHML wasn't all serious hard work, of course. We were always pulling pranks on each other, though one night one of the guys took it too far. I was reading a late-night newscast and he lit a pizza box on fire and threw it into the studio. He obviously forgot that the studio floors were cork, and in about two minutes the whole damned floor was on fire, flames leaping up. I could see the flames and smell the smoke, but I had to go on reading the newscast, trying not to let the listeners know there was anything going on. Suddenly I heard the door opening and then, to compound everything else he'd done, the pizza-box thrower started jumping up and down on the bloody box, trying to put the fire out. Everyone could now hear the noise this idiot was making in the studio because it was bouncing off the walls while I was still trying to keep the show together. We laughed for half an hour afterward.

My "baptism by fire" in the news-gathering end of the business came one night via a phone call from a contact in the police dispatch office. A few nights before, a man who was apparently deranged had bludgeoned his elderly parents to death. Then to cover his crime and finish the job, he had set fire to the family home and fled. The police had been scouring the city for him ever since. The call into the newsroom was to let me know he had finally been spotted downtown near the city hall, and the cops were on their way to pick him up. The message was "Get down there quickly if you want to score a scoop." I fairly flew. In fact, I got there seconds before the first police cruiser arrived. I jumped from the car and, with my tape recorder flung over my shoulder, headed for the block where the suspect had last been seen. I spotted him. But as I approached, he reached into the burlap sack he was carrying, pulled out what looked like a shotgun, turned the weapon toward his face and fired both barrels. I was stunned. His blood and parts of his head flew everywhere before he slumped to the pavement. I didn't sleep for nights after that, but I had earned my first badge in radio journalism.

As a reward I got to share the crime beat with another young guy by the name of Bill Sturrup who had begun his sports announcing career at age fifteen. Many people came to know him as the stadium announcer at Hamilton Tiger Cats CFL games, and he eventually earned the title "The Voice of Hamilton." When he died in January 2007, he was eulogized as one of the great contributors to Hamilton history, so good was he at mixing his long love of what he did at CHML with what he could do for his community. With Bill's help I gradually honed my skills, landing interviews with some of the notable and interesting people of the day. Yousuf Karsh was one of my favourites. He granted me some time in his Ottawa studios where his work was displayed everywhere. I was in awe. There, staring down at me, was Churchill with a smouldering cigar pinched between his fingers. The actor Peter Ustinov was on another wall. Diefenbaker was up there, too, and most of the other luminaries of the time had their places there as well. I think Karsh quickly sensed my inexperience, and he took over the situation, even suggested questions and for all intents and purposes interviewed himself. It was brilliant, and I was forever grateful. Bill and I, as associate editors/producers, sold the interview in two parts to the CBC Radio program *Assignment*. We were as proud as we could be. The corporation paid us all of fifty dollars.

It was during those days in Hamilton that I also met Harvey Kirck, the news anchor at the local TV station CHCH, another of Ken Soble's companies. It had been a CBC affiliate when he arrived there in 1960, but a year later it became the first independent television station in the country and soon part of the fledgling CTV Network. In late 1963 the network chose him to anchor the *CTV National News* and moved him to Ottawa where his first co-anchor was twenty-four-year-old Peter Jennings, then a fixture at CJOH-TV in Ottawa as the host of the dance-party program *Club Thirteen,* though he was destined for eventual fame as anchor of the ABC network news. Although producing the news from Ottawa placed CTV's reporters closer to the political action, within three years the network had moved Harvey Kirck and its main news production unit to CFTO-TV's studios in Toronto, and it was there that I met him again after I made my leap to television. We became good friends over the years and he was one of my first mentors. He was a big bear of a guy who loved to party but had an even greater love of snowmobile racing across the snowy countryside. Then one winter he made the mistake of combining the two and earned a place in the *Globe and Mail* after he was apprehended and accused of being in charge of his machine—more or less—while under the influence. Not much later he settled into the more serene world of boating on Lake Simcoe. Not that this excluded the party aspect of his life, but police boats were few and far between on that particular lake.

The day came when I had gone as far as I could at CHML, getting a solid grounding as a news writer, street reporter and news reader in an organization that carried itself collectively with integrity and pride. So out came my CV and my audition tapes to be updated and forwarded yet again. It may seem that broadcasters then were nomads, wandering from place to place, never settling for long and often moving for nothing more than a better paycheque. But that was the way of our world at the time. We picked our opportunities based on what was available and what was offered, but as there wasn't much point in making lateral moves, we picked the main chance whenever it came. The industry was still in its formative stages, licences were being assigned by the Board of Broadcast Governors (the forerunner of today's Canadian Radio and Television Commission) on a more frequent basis, so as the job market widened, we kept our eyes peeled and our resumes at hand—just in case. The game was always on.

At that time most people in the business considered Toronto to be, in a mocking sense, the centre of the universe. Nevertheless, it was the market just about all of us had our sights on. And the market leader there was CHUM—the very model of a successful rock and roll radio station—and it had a top-of-the-line news operation. I desperately wanted to work there, but the news director was a curmudgeonly old legend named Bill Drylie who demanded and inevitably received absolute loyalty and obedience to an arbitrary set of rules he had conceived over the years. One of those rules was that no staff member was allowed, under pain of firing, to wear a suit coat while on shift. After Drylie hired me—much to my surprise—I inadvertently set the tone for our relationship by telling him his dress code meant nothing to me because I always worked in a jacket. He grunted a threat about a possibly short career at CHUM if I didn't work in shirtsleeves, and from then on we were destined not to get along. Maybe that was why I was always assigned the late shift long after Drylie had left for the day.

The upside of my experience at CHUM was working with great talent like Bob McAdorey with whom I had also worked a few years earlier in Guelph, Peter Dickens, Taylor Parnaby and Jungle Jay Nelson, a transplanted American from Buffalo, who ruled the morning airwaves in Toronto. In a very short time I learned a lot from these guys, even how to counter the attentions of the public who, because we worked at sidewalk level in what was essentially a fishbowl, would press their noses against the window and taunt us. The others taught me to assume that the intruders probably couldn't read our lips and, if we moved our mouths fast enough, we could send them reeling on their way, chastised and confused. And they also taught me how to party. In fact, their carousing was the stuff legends are made of, with most of it occurring, during my time there at least, in rented rooms at the King Edward Hotel. More than one morning I got to bed at seven and went to work a little later in the day with a hangover the size of a Volkswagen.

Rye and ginger, the entry-level drink of the day for aspiring party animals, could have devastating results and often did.

My job at CHUM didn't last long—not because of any bad blood between myself and news director Drylie but because after only five months in that job television came calling and I took the escape route. The opportunity to leave came about because Joe Mariash, a colleague during my radio days in Hamilton who was now working at CFTO–TV as a news anchor and reporter, knew that his boss, Doug Johnston, who doubled as the news director and the six o'clock anchor, was in the market for a junior-level reporter. Joe suggested that Johnston should take a look at me, and Johnston called me at CHUM to suggest that we meet for lunch. During that phone conversation he told me that he liked my radio work and then added, "If you look as good as you sound, you'll do well out here." The "out here" meant Agincourt on the outskirts of Toronto where CFTO is located.

We had lunch down the street from the radio station at the Ports of Call restaurant where I remember they served those awful-looking drinks concocted with blue curacao and gin and topped with little umbrellas. Johnston was a big, robust, happy man, and unlike my previous boss he had a sense of humour. We hit it off right away and I learned that he had apparently been scouting me for a while. We chatted in general terms about the new medium before he explained his expectations for its growth and how I might fit in. His excitement ignited mine and within an hour we shook hands on a deal. I would join his staff as a street reporter. There was no mention of my chances of becoming a news anchor, and frankly I was just happy to be moving away from a situation that had lost its charm for me. Anchoring, if it was ever to be something I would do, hadn't entered my mind—yet.

I was happy to snap up the job because at that time there weren't many offers coming from TV stations as there were so few of them, and the money was better than what I was getting. I also knew from Joe Mariash that the newsroom at CFTO was on a learning curve, and I could be part of that process. During my short tenure at CHUM Radio in Toronto, television news operations had really started to grow. They had basically started with fifteen-minute, bulletin-style coverage of events and were now switching to a thirty-minute format that included weather forecasts and sports news; as a result, they were becoming a journalistic force to be reckoned with. So I put on my best suit jacket, went to Bill Drylie's office and kissed off radio for the last time. I counted myself lucky to be heading into television.

The CFTO Years

In 1958 THE FOWLER COMMISSION on broadcasting had recommended that the CBC give up its role as the industry's regulator, and a year later a new body, the Board of Broadcast Governors (BBG), was given the power to regulate radio and television across the country. One of the board's first acts was to announce that it would accept applications for a licence to set up and operate a private television station in Toronto. A new company called Baton Broadcasting, owned by John Bassett and John David Eaton (who were co-owners of the *Toronto Telegram*) was one of the first contenders for the new licence, but by the time the BBG's hearings opened in March 1960, Baton had joined forces with a second contender, Aldred Rogers Broadcasting, to become Baton Aldred Rogers Broadcasting. The company brought in Rai Purdy, a Canadian who had put Scottish Television on air for Roy Thomson, and Purdy designed a complete program for the proposed station, CFTO, composed mostly of live shows with a strong news and sports component. It was a recipe that won them the licence, and CFTO went on the air on the last day of December 1960 from studios in the *Toronto Telegram* building. These studios would remain the station's city news site, though within a year the main station was housed in a new complex called Channel Nine Court on a twenty-acre parcel of land in the wilds of Agincourt. Meanwhile, Spence Caldwell, one of the unsuccessful applicants for the Toronto television licence, was attempting—without much luck—to form a network of all the new private stations across the country, but his luck changed after CFTO won the broadcast rights to the Canadian Football League Eastern Conference games and needed a network to make those rights profitable. Caldwell was at last able to make a deal, and his CTV Television Network was launched on October 1, 1961, linking seven independent stations across the country, though CFTO was the network's flagship.

Beyond the obvious—the visual aspect of the medium—there was one main difference between radio and television that took a lot of getting used to. In radio I had been a one-man operation—just me and my tape recorder. Granted, at the time tape recorders were enormous machines, cumbersome, heavy and only portable, as one of my Ryerson instructors was fond of saying, "if you have a ten-ton truck." In television I became a player in a band. There was the reporter, the camera operator (nowadays called the shooter), a sound technician and sometimes a producer. The last two were eventually trimmed by most news operations due to budget considerations or technological advances, after which the reporter was often pressed into extra service to fill in the gaps. As a street reporter I got used to this system, even became good at it, but it was still a big adjustment.

In the CFTO newsroom I found myself working with a totally professional group of writers and reporters dedicated to making "the product" the best it could be. There wasn't much competition in those days, just the local CBC outlet, but they were a challenge if only because of the breadth of their resources and their head start. We ploughed along doing the best we could, relying heavily on what the newspapers were reporting on any given day. In fact, by picking up the *Globe and Mail* and checking out the front page on my way to the office, I could guess with a reasonable amount of certainty what story or stories I would be covering for the nightly newscast. We originated very few stories of our own at that time, and investigative reporting had not yet been invented. Still, it made for a presentable broadcast and it seemed to come together at a reasonable cost—the price of a few newspapers—though that changed in years to come. (Later when I began working for BCTV, we discovered that both the *Province* and *Sun* newspapers monitored our show every night to see what, if anything, we had that they might have missed. Often we led the way in those situations.) My initial reporting duties at CFTO were the kind usually doled out to the newest staff members. The order from the assignment desk came as often as not in a terse command: "Go and talk to so-and-so and ask him about such-and-such"—in other words, "Bring me back a talking head," as they were called. I was even given a list of questions to put to the newsmaker. Sometimes I arrived back at the station with three or four of these "heads" dangling from my belt. Not much in the way of substance but enough to fill some holes in the content of the six o'clock news. I suppose my bosses were thinking: We know he can handle words, but how about words and pictures together?

It could only get better for me, and soon I was trusted with bigger stuff, told to do "stand-ups," to wrap the talking heads with more information and to flesh out the story with facts I might have discovered for myself. Actual reporting. And even to originate stories based on my own ideas—"think pieces" we called them. Over time I earned my stripes, and the whole experience became filled with excitement for me. I travelled to the Sudbury area to report on the retirement of the last doctor in a small, impoverished northern Ontario mining town, then farther afield to talk to labour leaders about current or impending strikes that might cripple the local economy. I went into the tobacco fields to report on that year's crop and to Newfoundland to spend time with Joey Smallwood as he reminisced about his province's entry into Confederation.

Eventually I was launched on a cross-Canada reporting tour—just me and a cameraman, self-assigning but open to suggestions. We began in the Maritimes and worked our way to Alberta. We looked at life on the fishing grounds and in the outports of Newfoundland and reported on the burgeoning growth of Halifax, the survival of the old section of Quebec City and the aftermath of Expo 67 in Montreal. We ended in Hobbema, Alberta, in the foothills of the Rockies to tell the story of a disgruntled Native group intent on preserving the old ways against the incursion of new people, mostly white, who wanted to resettle the land, expand development and bring in their version of civilization. While the protestors seemed accepting of my presence at first, they became a little grumpy as time passed, and I began to feel none too comfortable among them. It was winter and icy cold, and only the arrival of a Chinook wind helped make the experience bearable. I decided to hit the road as soon as I filed my story.

Finally I was given a permanent spot on weekends, presenting the Saturday and Sunday versions of *Nightbeat*. My on-air partner delivering the sports news was Annis Stukus, who was even then something of a legend in Canadian football circles, and rightly so. In 1935 he had joined the Toronto Argonauts and spent seven seasons as a star quarterback, place-kicker and all-round back, leading them to Grey Cup victories in 1937 and '38. But "Stuke" was carrying around a second career as a reporter and broadcaster, starting back in 1929 when at fifteen he landed a job as a copy boy with the *Toronto Star*; by 1941 he was back there writing sports, though he still played football with minor teams until 1946. Three years later he went off to Edmonton to coach, manage and promote the Canadian Football League's new Eskimos football franchise; he helped that team reach the western finals in 1951 and '52. The next year he was recruited to be head coach and spokesman for yet another fresh CFL franchise, the new BC Lions in Vancouver. After three years he returned to his media life as football editor for the *Vancouver Sun,* but in 1960 John Bassett and family lured him east again to become a columnist for the *Toronto Telegram* and a sports commentator for CFTO. When we shared a studio at CFTO in 1970, he had just spent two years as general manager of the early version of the Vancouver Canucks hockey team when they were members of the Western Hockey League.

When I stepped to the podium on the night of my maiden TV broadcast, my only thought was survival, as in don't-collapse-on-the-studio-floor-before-you-get-through-this-ordeal! The format called for us to stand during the show, and I made my way shakily through the first couple of stories, but it was clear to me that at any moment my career would end before it began and I'd be back on the street working a beat. But Stuke sensed my plight, and during the first commercial break he walked up to me, leaned down (I'm short and he was very big), put one of his huge arms around my shoulders and said simply, "It's okay, kid, you can make it. You've got the stuff." It was just the right thing to say at the right moment. I took a huge breath and carried on to the end of the show. I will always be grateful for his gesture. After he became sports director for CFUN Radio in 1975, we ran into each other at a charity function and I thanked him again. He said he couldn't remember the incident. When he died at age ninety-one in Canmore, Alberta, in 2006, the whole thing jumped back into my mind and I silently said "thanks" one more time.

The name of our show—*Nightbeat*—was, by the way, a

direct steal from a late-night interview show fronted by Mike Wallace in 1956 for the small television station WABD in New York, just before he went to work for CBS. It was on that show that he developed his technique for those edgy interviews he specialized in with the good guys and bad guys who were the newsmakers of the day. Then, as now, Wallace pulled no punches, and his ambush style became his awesome trademark. On our version of *Nightbeat* there was no cutting edge, just straightforward recitations of the day's events, but it was a good place to start for someone still trying to find his feet in the business.

Stuke and I attracted our fair share of viewers, but as I recall, we were pretty much the only game in town at that time of night on a weekend, so if you wanted a news summary, weather or sports results, you flipped over to us. If nothing else, it gave me a chance to show the viewers and management what I could do, and I got fairly good reviews. At the same time I was keeping up my reporting duties during the week, only now, with my emerging recognition as an on-air personality, I had the clout I needed to call my own shots and pick the stories I might actually have some fun with, stories that went beyond the regular daily agenda. Feature stories, I guess you could call them. This had the added benefit of keeping me out of the line of fire of some editor who wanted an interview with the grieving parents of a missing child or a tragically maimed accident victim, or a "reaction piece" to some new Queen's Park legislation. Or even, heaven help me, a man-on-the-street piece on what the editor thought was a life-changing issue in law, politics or economics. I hated, as I think most TV reporters do, stopping people on the street, shoving a microphone and camera in their faces and, more often than not, getting turned down flat. People will throw themselves into heavy traffic, rushing across a busy street to the opposite sidewalk, just to get away from nosey reporters. The process usually ends with about four, never more than five, opinions actually finding their way to air. It's an exasperating ordeal for the reporter, though a potent weapon in the hands of some grumpy assignment editor who might not have liked your story in yesterday's lineup and wants to show you that, despite your salary being higher than his and his anonymity as a "behind the scenes" player, he can still make your life miserable.

Some days on the job were made more frustrating by technology—or the lack thereof—because those were the days of film, as opposed to the videotape used now. The problem with shooting on film was that you never knew what you were bringing back to the station. Then you had to wait for the film to be developed, and if you weren't the first reporter to deliver film that afternoon, you were slotted into a lineup that made for more time consumed. When you finally got your hands on it and could sit down with a film editor to look at it, you were hit by the realization of what a crapshoot it was. The film could have been scratched and rendered unusable by some problem with the camera or the soundtrack might be scratchy or non-existent. You ended up cobbling it together as best you could, but without some of the necessary elements to make the story fly. And there was no going back. If you had interviewed the prime minister, for example—and it might have been an exclusive face-to-face—your chances of getting him to do it all over again were absolutely nil. In any case, you'd probably be too embarrassed to admit that the triumph of the day had disintegrated in a film lab.

Ask a cameraperson what it was like to work in those days in terms of the equipment's weight and size, and they'll tell you about the back problems brought on by toting a forty- or fifty-pound camera around. All these problems are now greatly alleviated by much lighter, less cumbersome, almost foolproof video cameras. Now you can check your interviews the moment after you ask your final question and sign off on picture quality before you leave the location. You can even edit your piece in a mobile, a truck with microwave or satellite capabilities, and send the finished product to the station without having to drive the sometimes long trip back to the studio. There aren't many downsides to this type of technology that I can determine except that it displaced personnel, and when they're your friends, that's never an acceptable thing.

On the set at CFTO most of the problems that occurred were technical glitches that nobody had any control over— a piece of equipment would break down, a camera would wander off on its own and show a part of the studio that the viewers weren't supposed to see. But sometimes the glitches were caused by human failings. I remember that there was a big break between the end of the half-hour six o'clock news show and the beginning of the late news, which started at 11:15 or 11:30, so the camera guys would take the break at the local Legion. One night they came back so drunk that they were falling asleep behind the cameras. In fact, they couldn't stand up let alone run a television camera.

They drank on the job as well but covered it a little better, mostly because the entrances to most studios in those days had airlocks for sound purposes. These consisted of two doors that closed on each other, and I'll never forget the time we were undergoing studio renovations and a workman opened up one of these seldom-used airlocks. Out came a rain of beer and liquor bottles and cans. They had filled it up by opening the door and quickly tossing them in, and eventually there was a six-foot mound in there, and it all came pouring out on one of these poor working guys.

Another time at CFTO, I was sitting in the studio just about to go on air when a workman came in with a bucket of paint and a brush and started painting the set. I had about thirty seconds to air, and I said, "What the hell are you doing?"

He said, "I was told to come in here and paint the set."

I said, "I don't really think they meant during the time I'm on the air!"

But he started painting anyway.

Finally I just yelled, "Go away! Go away!"

Of course, he had misunderstood. Somebody had told him that the set had to be painted and he thought he meant right then. We all laughed about it afterward.

In time I settled comfortably into the dual role of reporter and anchor, and my life at CFTO became fun and exciting—and even rewarding in the sense of financial compensation. I remember discussing it with my brother John and telling him enthusiastically that my annual salary was at a giddying peak. They were paying me ten thousand dollars a year to do something I thoroughly enjoyed. "Ten thousand," John said. "My God, that's a fortune!" I believed that it was, too, and I didn't know how much better things could get.

Despite the money I was making, I became restless at CFTO. Fortunately, about that time my old friend Joe Mariash, who had been instrumental in getting me the job in the first place, decided to move on. He'd had an offer from the Shell Oil Company to take over a public relations spot and decided to leave his anchor job on television for the corporate world. And despite what the general manager might have thought about me—he actually said that I looked too Italian to be successful on air—I was tapped as Joe's successor.

Shortly after that, our news director and six o'clock newscaster, Doug Johnston, left the station for the biggies (the local ABC station in New York), and his job went to Ken Cavanagh, a delightful man with bona fide credentials as a journalist. He had held down a job at the CBC, working, I think, in their news and documentary division until the day in 1966 that our parent network CTV created *W5*, and they asked Ken to be one of the on-air hosts. It was then, as now, a *60 Minutes/Dateline* hybrid but with strictly Canadian content. As well as hosting *W5*, Ken was given the dual role in our local operation that Doug Johnston had abandoned. He toughed his way through the six o'clock news every night, but he had problems with the administrative side of the news director's responsibilities because he was just too kind to all of us problem-makers in the newsroom. As well, his heritage weighed heavily on the Irish side, and I always thought that the way he lived his life was tantamount to an "Irish death wish." Finally, his approach to discipline and budgets became more than the so-called suits could take, and he was ousted from the daily news program and the news director's office, though not from *W5*.

As far as CFTO was concerned, it was goodbye Ken, hello Ted Stuebing. Ted had been a print guy, and I had first run across him during my days working out of the *Toronto Telegram* building, which had remained CFTO's downtown base. To my recollection he had not been a standout reporter and had spent most of his time riding a desk in the editorial department, so I was surprised (as were many others) when he was chosen to replace Cavanagh. I was even more surprised when he brought along, as his second-in-command, another newspaper-type named Jim Bard, who also had no experience in our domain. Even in those days, of course, there was a decided animosity between print and electronic journalists. The print journalists looked upon us with great disdain; they believed we were just prima donnas. We thought they were snobbish, know-it-all braggarts who had no understanding of our place in the journalistic pecking order and no idea what we did. On top of that Ted was more or less devoid of a sense of humour and, in my estimation, certainly appeared to have no leadership qualities whatsoever. Instead, he used his tall, imposing stature to keep the newsroom people in line and coped coldly with whatever stress he might have felt. Admittedly, we didn't make it easy for him.

Bard, on the other hand, came across as being a little more human than his boss. You could at least argue about an issue with him without feeling you were hitting your head against a wall. But we all knew (or at least suspected) that Stuebing had brought him along to be his henchman, a role I think Bard grew to detest. I believe to this day that he would much rather have been in the trenches with the reporting staff he was hired to ride herd on. His one distinguishing feature was a clipboard he carried with him wherever he went. I was never quite sure what he used it for. Come to think of it, I can't ever remember seeing him use it. It was just there. It might have been a prop, his version of a sign of authority.

From the very first day Stuebing encamped in the news director's office, things went badly for him. He ran up against a barricade of disrespect and resentment, and he handled it by becoming more of a bully than a leader. I think he really wanted to be "one of the boys," to make friends, but he couldn't bring himself down to our level. In what in retrospect seems to be a childish reaction to the new regime, someone among the staff took it upon himself to buy several spray cans of "cobwebs," the kind you find in stores around Halloween, and completely cover Ted's office with the stuff. Then someone Crazy Glued the receivers to the bases of the phones in Stuebing's office and to others in offices belonging to people deemed to be Stuebing loyalists. Pat Marsden, CFTO's legendary sports director, went after Stuebing, too, but in a much more physical way. During a tirade Stuebing was delivering on Marsden's inability to run the sports department as Stuebing wanted it run, Marsden hurled himself across the desk and went in for the kill. Fortunately, he was too short to make it all the way and fell just shy of his target. But this stormy exchange ended Marsden's nineteen-year television career and landed him back in radio at CFRB and later at The Fan Sports Radio station.

This was the kind of stuff that created legends in the broadcasting business in those days, but by the summer of 1973 I was fed up with the nonsense. I was doing fairly well, staying out of the news director's way, doing my evening shift without much direct interference, but the atmosphere, even under those circumstances, soon became unbearable, and I decided to look around for something to do elsewhere. My first thought was to go to England and land a job with the BBC. I took some holidays, made the trip and checked with a few of my contacts in London, but the one or two offers I received and the salaries involved fell short of what I thought I was due. However, I came back to Canada and the CFTO newsroom just as determined to make a move, and that's when the idea of becoming a CTV network correspondent struck me. I knew there were people at CTV who respected my work on air and as a reporter, so one day in the winter of 1973–74 I asked for an appointment with Tom Gould, the head of the news and public affairs department down on Charles Street in Toronto. He was more enthusiastic than I dared hope about the possibility and went so far as to tell me that it was about time I gave up on the on-air job while I still had the legs to be a reporter. But I cooled immediately on the idea when he offered me the job of bureau chief in Halifax. I had spent a few days there during my roving assignment days with CFTO and had not liked it one bit. "No thanks," I remember saying, "but if anything comes up in Vancouver, I'd like to be considered." It was a completely random call on my part; I had plucked the city's name out of the blue. I had never been to the West Coast and knew nothing about the city. But we left it at that and I went back to CFTO.

It must have been less than a month later that I got the phone call from Gould that literally changed my entire life. As fate would have it, there had been a falling-out between the lead correspondent in British Columbia, Casey Baldwin, and his Toronto bosses. Baldwin was ordered home and I was being considered as his replacement in the two-man West Coast bureau. In no time at all Gould and I had agreed to a deal, and I had given my notice to Ted Stuebing, who appeared entirely unfazed by my resignation. In fact, he did everything but help me pack. I guess I was just one more thorn eased out of his side.

CTV Network Correspondent in Vancouver

On the morning in April 1974 that my wife and I left Toronto, the temperature was cold even by Toronto standards. The city was still in the grip of another long and tiresome winter, and this, of course, was one more thing that had helped me decide to make the move to Vancouver. I also knew I would not miss the unbearably hot, humid Ontario summers. An airline strike had complicated our travel plans that day, and we had to fly to Seattle, Washington, and rent a car to drive up to Vancouver. When we boarded the plane, we were bundled up in heavy winter jackets, but when we got to Seattle the world had changed—at least in terms of the weather. Men were in shirtsleeves, women were wearing light dresses and jackets. The drive north to

Vancouver was sublime, and I knew at last that I had really done the right thing.

In order to make the transition from East to West a little smoother, my wife had made a flying visit to Vancouver a few weeks earlier to find a place to rent. Her choice was a good one—a small house in Deep Cove overlooking Indian Arm, a beautiful stretch of fjord-like water. The location of the house and the temperate climate, despite long spells of rain, sealed it for me. I couldn't think of a better place to work or live.

After a short break to get used to my surroundings, I launched into my new career as a national news correspondent and bureau chief. That last part was not, by any means, a big deal. Although the CTV Network had been established for thirteen years, their news-gathering machine was just beginning to grind into motion. My "bureau" was a small room in our house, and the equipment consisted of a desk, a typewriter and a phone. I added a bookcase and a few reference manuals to make it look a little grander, but it was still a home office. Looking back, I realize that the phone might have been a mistake because the editors and assignment managers back in Toronto often seemed to lose track of time zones. More often than not, they would call me at eight in the morning eastern time when their day was already in high gear, expecting me to be alert and keen. It never seemed to occur to them that on the West Coast, not a lawyer, politician or newsmaker of any other kind— except perhaps bad women and burglars—was stirring yet. It took me a while to convince them that there really was a three-hour time difference between their offices and my BC outpost. That minor problem aside, however, life became much more interesting and exciting than it had been at CFTO.

The other man in our two-man bureau was Len Kowalewich, one of the most competent cameramen I have ever worked with, and even though we had our differences over the years, he is someone I still count as a friend, someone who taught me a lot about taking raw material from the camera and turning it into a viable story. For the most part, Len and I could be more or less self-assigning, and our first story together dealt with a longshoremen's strike that was, as they say, "down and dirty." In the final story there was less than a minute of me, just a head and shoulders shot, explaining the economic impact on the city and its reputation as a port if the dispute was to go on for any amount of time. I didn't think it was much of a debut on my part, but the next day when I picked up my mail at the CTV affilate station CHAN-TV (a year later it would adopt the unofficial call sign BCTV), there was a memo from Craig Oliver (my immediate boss then and now known across the country as the network's long-serving chief Ottawa correspondent), saying how "impressive" it was. If that's the case, I remember thinking, this could be the beginning of a really easy job. And at times it was.

The one hitch in my relationship with Len was centred around his family background. His father, as I recall, had been a member of the Communist Party of Canada during the family's days in Winnipeg, and as a result Len, by association, was not allowed to cross the border into the US. This put a crimp in some of our efforts because, whenever a story came up in some part of the States that was considered our territory, I had to dig deep into my meagre bureau budget and hire a replacement. Although he often joked about it, I think Len was deeply hurt by this edict from some faceless bureaucrat in Washington and slightly resentful about someone taking over his job, if only on an occasional basis.

More than a few times I plucked Don Timbrell out of the CHAN-TV lineup and used him on stories Len was not allowed to handle. His professionalism was on the same level as Len's, and he worked hard and well. But there came a day when he probably wished he'd been passed over just this once. Washington State and part of southern BC are situated within the so-called Ring of Fire, a circle of dormant volcanoes, one of which decided to become active again and rumbled back to life. Mount Baker, which until then had been a benign geographical standout and ski destination just across the BC–Washington border, began hissing gas, smoke and ash one late spring day in 1975. This raised fears that the volcano's rising heat could melt its glaciers and cause catastrophic mud flows, so the Baker Lake area was evacuated. I immediately hooked up with Timbrell to cover the story. It couldn't be done properly, I thought, without aerial shots, and I began looking for a helicopter, but just about every other news service was ahead of me. We had to settle for a small, fixed-wing aircraft from an airport not far from the mountain. Don knew how important these shots would be, so I convinced him to get the pilot to take the doors off the plane so there would be nothing but clear shots of the spewing mountain. No problem.

Well, no problem for me, anyway. I stayed on the ground to attack some of the other angles of the story. An hour or so later Don was back, decidedly green in complexion but certain he'd got all the film he needed. I thought perhaps he had inhaled too much sulphur or whatever from the plumes of smoke and gases emitting from the volcano. "No, nothing like that," he confided in me. "I just hate flying." I had sent this poor guy and his phobia into the mountains with a pilot he didn't know—and a plane he certainly didn't care for—to shoot through an empty doorway thousands of feet in the air. I don't think he ever forgot that ride.

My new job took me to many more places and events I never knew existed. Within the first few weeks I had filed stories on a killer-whale census, the near-riots and rowdyism brought on by labour disagreements, elections and by-elections, conflicts involving Native land claims, and even the 1974 Grey Cup, held in a rain-soaked Empire Stadium, between the Montreal Alouettes and the Edmonton Eskimos. (Alouettes won 20–7.) That last event, by the way, led to my co-hosting the CTV Network morning show *Canada AM* when it travelled to the West Coast to feed off the football hoopla. It was the network's opportunity to identify me as the new bureau chief, but I was not ready to play with the pros. I muddled through a couple of mornings, but it was painful both for me and the regular hosts and their producers. I felt uncomfortable and entirely out of my element as I'm not a great ad-libber at the best of times and need the security of notes or a teleprompter. And back then my interviewing skills still needed a lot of shoring up. By nature I'm a reticent man, and I think it takes someone with a much more outgoing personality to be part of the front team on programs such as *Canada AM,* which feature long-style interviews, host participation in cooking and craft segments and general, breezy banter between the main characters. Another time I substituted for Jack Webster on his daily talk show. It was one morning only and not, I'll tell you, to critical acclaim. I was just a better reporter than performer, even though the two roles are often tied together. I think I'm better at it now, but in those days it was a strain.

During that same "breaking in" period as CTV's West Coast bureau chief, I was expected to become the eyes and ears for the federal election coverage out here. My role on election night, July 8, 1974, was to report on the various races in BC and how the vote count might tip the balance for any of the parties. The problem was, as I saw it, that by the time the polls closed in the West, the electorate in the East—meaning Quebec and Ontario—had usually decided the race, and we were left to "bat cleanup," as it were. I did my reporting from Toronto that night, manning a desk dedicated to my geographical responsibility, and read results generated by computers, which up to that time had not been widely used in vote counting. Previous election broadcasts had been powered by actual people receiving numbers by phone from the various ridings, passing them to other people who posted them in large felt-pen letters on huge result boards positioned around the studio. It seems crude now, but watching the numbers change manually gave you a chance to see "horse races" develop in what are now called "battleground ridings." It brought an element of suspense to the proceedings.

And on that 1974 election night in Toronto we were suddenly left wishing for the old days when without warning the computers crashed—as they sometimes did in those days—taking with them our ability to report anything from anywhere. Weeks of preparation had gone into this night and we watched it collapse around us in seconds. We had to resort to paper, and the program finished in a shambles with the guys at CBC, I'm sure, laughing at our misfortune. Just as there was competition among the political parties, the networks also squared off against each other, hoping to win the night in terms of viewership. My most poignant memory of that night was the sight of our producer, Tim Kotcheff, sitting alone in the darkened studio long after the show was over, hammering at his computer in an attempt to bring everything back to life. It didn't work. It was over. And I remember thinking how like the Phantom of the Opera he looked, alone and forlorn. Unfortunately, in the post-mortem that followed, Tim carried most of the blame for the program coming down around our ears, even though the computer wizards who had worked with him to set the system up had assured him nothing could go wrong, go wrong, go wrong, go wrong—as the old joke goes.

From then on, though, my life as a reporter became a flurry of travel and excitement. Even fun. There were days when Len and I would rise early in Vancouver, head out to the airport and then to some place like Whitehorse or the northern areas of British Columbia and spend a couple of days scouting out stories. We would keep in constant touch with the newsroom in Toronto, getting them revved up over something we planned to file according to our schedule and time zone and not their agenda. Being our own assignment editor had its benefits. We tried to keep our stories timeless but interesting, never ignoring those events that had a national urgency.

A couple of those stories immediately come to mind. Native blockades were a common event then—the seventy-one-day siege at Wounded Knee in South Dakota had occurred just the previous year and Natives had occupied Anicinabe Park near Kenora, Ontario, just months earlier. We covered a few in BC, including one near Cache Creek in 1974 that led to my confrontation with a lone Native guard carrying a rifle. Len and I saw him as we approached a barricade put up to stop unwanted intrusions on the disputed land. He was alone and seemed a little bit sleepy, but he was armed and I had no way of knowing his disposition at the time. In some kind of uncharacteristic show of bravado I told Len to keep his camera running while I approached the man on foot and tried to get him to talk. As I got closer, I got a better look at the weapon he held. It was a .22 calibre rifle but it was obviously old and neglected. Rust streaked down the barrel and I doubt if it could have been fired. He raised it to eye level and kept it there as I tried to explain to him who we were and why we were there. Then I saw him glance over my shoulder where he must have caught a glimpse of the camera and understood right away he had been "caught," if only on film, and he lowered his rifle to explain that he was only doing his job as defined by his elders and he meant no harm. I don't want to make more of it than it was because it's not as if I was some combat-ready soldier doing duty in a wartorn foreign country, but later when the possible danger of the situation sank in, I collapsed into the van thinking that I probably should not do that kind of thing again. It did, however, make our story on that local issue much more dramatic.

A similar story took us up to Pemberton, where Lil'wat Native people had closed the vital Duffy Lake Road to get attention for their land claims. The standoff understandably upset local residents who wanted to go north from their small town because they were forced to make a huge detour south through the Whistler ski resort area and Squamish, then on through the outskirts of Vancouver before turning north again through the Fraser Canyon. As a result, it didn't take long for the RCMP to get involved, and they marshalled every morning in Pemberton to plan an approach to settling the affair quickly and without breaking heads. While they watched and waited, we took our camera to the front line to talk to the protest leaders to see if they had a plan of action. But they were taking a similar watch and wait stance, so Len and I settled in somewhere between the two factions to see what would develop. We went back and forth between them, filing daily reports and to a certain extent becoming friends with the alleged offenders—and for that matter the law enforcers—and possibly choosing sides, something I've always said a journalist should not do. The day came when the Mounties made their move, heading into the area to dismantle the barricade and open the road. As everything came tumbling down on the protestors, they resorted to a defiant sit-in. It was short-lived.

The police scooped sixty-three of them up one by one, but gently, and loaded them on to a waiting bus.

Because I had breached that journalistic boundary between objectivity and subjectivity, the moment caught me off guard. Tears welled up in my eyes as I saw the men and women carried away, one officer holding their arms, another their legs. And something flashed through my mind about "man's inhumanity to man."

My role as CTV's West Coast bureau chief ended within eight months of my move to the West Coast, the direct result of a disagreement with my boss in Toronto, Don Cameron, over what I was being paid. I had come west for sixteen thousand dollars a year, but I soon realized that with the cost of living out here this was not enough. The money issue was compounded by the fact that I was the lone correspondent with this huge territory and I was already getting a little tired of travelling and working with the different time zones. All the travelling hadn't helped my marriage either, though we tried to keep it going, even buying our own home on Keith Road in West Vancouver— the first house I had ever owned—but the marriage was already essentially over.

About five months into my job with CTV, I had contacted Don Cameron and said, "I can't live out here on what you're paying me. I need a raise."

His response was, "I'll think about it."

In the meantime, Cameron Bell, who was the CHAN-TV

news director, knew I wasn't having a good time with CTV, and he came to me one day to ask, "Would you consider anchoring our six o'clock show?"

I said, "Let me work this out. I really feel I need to give the network some time to come back to me on this."

Another two or three months went by and then Don Cameron got back to me with "I've thought about it, and we can't afford any more than that."

"Well, gee," I said, "I hope you don't mind if I look around and see what else is going on?"

"Help yourself," Don said.

So then I told Cameron Bell, "Let's talk." And by the time the two of us had walked around the block, I said, "Okay, fine. I'm your man."

Life as a BCTV News Anchor

BCTV BEGAN LIFE as Channel 8—or CHAN-TV—Vancouver's first independent television station, on October 31, 1960, in temporary studios at 1219 Richards Street, the address of a photography studio belonging to Art Jones, one of the principals in Vantel Broadcasting, which had won the Vancouver television licence. Initially the station's signal was so poor that it could only be seen in the city's downtown core and even there it was inferior to the CBC signal and that of KVOS in Bellingham, Washington. But in 1962 Channel 8 moved into permanent quarters just down the hill from the station's transmitter on Burnaby Mountain. Within eight years the new channel had extended its coverage via rebroadcast transmitters to the Fraser Valley and then to the Okanagan and two years after that to the Cariboo. By 1976 it could also be seen on the north coast and in the Kootenays, and by that time this CTV affiliate had adopted the unofficial call sign BCTV.

My deal with Cameron Bell when I started with CHAN-TV in early 1975 was that I would combine a little reporting with my anchoring duties, so I could do some stories I had chosen myself. One was about a Native man in Kamloops who supplied wild horses to rodeos—I recall that one of his horses was called Porch Climber. This fellow was getting on in years and retiring from the business so I did a really nice nostalgic piece on him with music backing it, a feature report. I followed that with a story on the sudden demise of a bunch of mountain sheep in the Okanagan. And after that I shot the Hell's Gate Rapids with a guy from Grant's Pass, Oregon. But it wasn't long before I got so involved in the daily news and the *News Hour* that I just stopped doing reporting.

There's no doubt in my mind that the success of the *News Hour* can be attributed to the ideas and foresight of four people. The first is Ray Peters, since 1954 a force in Canadian broadcasting. In 1961 he became managing director of Vantel Broadcasting (later renamed the Westcom TV Group), which included BCTV and Victoria's CHEK-TV, and turned its ailing fortunes around in less than three years. One of the biggest factors in that turnaround was his gamble that a nightly one-hour newscast on BCTV would pull in viewers and advertisers. To make it work, that newscast had to beat the viewership of Walter Cronkite's nightly newscast carried by KVOS in Bellingham, which was allowed to solicit advertising from clients on our side of the border, thereby taking revenue away from Canadian stations. That, for Peters, was simply putting money in the wrong pockets and he wanted an end to it.

On top of that, he had been involved in a hassle with the CTV Network over placement of the national newscast, arguing that it should have a presence at six o'clock. Move the current broadcast, he suggested in the strongest possible terms, or create a new package for the supper hour. When no one else around the CTV boardroom table bought the idea, Peters decided to go it alone and came up with what is now one of the most successful local news programs in North America. It was not long after its inception that the *News Hour* surpassed Walter Cronkite in the nightly ratings, and when broadcast regulations were finally changed, KVOS was forced to pull up stakes in Canada and source its revenue on its home ground.

Ray Peters moved from the day-to-day management of the Westcom TV Group in 1977 to become the president and CEO of the parent company, Western International Communications (WIC), and then retired from that post in 1989. Although we have very little contact these days, I still count him among my dearest friends. He was my mentor, in all senses of the word. He could be gruff with me if he thought I was falling short of my contract expectations or complained too loudly about some real or perceived problem in the newsroom, but he always took the time to listen. Over the years we negotiated an agreement or two by simply hooking up for lunch at the Vancouver Club, that downtown hangout for well-heeled business types. The atmosphere there borders on stodgy, and I was never quite comfortable in it, but looking back, it was quite an amazing event. I would show up. We'd chit-chat. He would ask me if I wanted to stay on at BCTV. I would say of course. He would tell me what the company was prepared to put in my next contract. I'd say okay. We would have a light lunch and leave. As simple as that. Some time after Ray left BCTV for the rarified atmosphere of the president's office at Western International Communications, my friend Paul Shaw became my negotiator, crossing swords with a succession of managers at the station and always doing well on my behalf. But I missed those lunches with Ray.

In the beginning Al Clapp led the way on the *News Hour* on a day-to-day basis. My first glimpse of him branded him forever in my mind as an aging hippie—the beard, the jeans and denim jacket and the hyper personality—but behind that façade he was a thinker and an innovator and he bristled with ideas. Not all of them were good, but some of them pushed the show to new heights. I particularly remember him for one especially innovative touch at BCTV. The very first day I went into the newsroom as the CTV correspondent, I had to swing open a battered screen door, the kind you find keeping out the summer's abundance of flies and mosquitoes on every Ontario and Prairie farmhouse. This was Al's idea, I was told. I wondered why, since the province is not known for its insect population, at least not in the Lower Mainland, and the newsroom was located along a dimly lit corridor in the basement of the building and didn't even have windows. I never did find out why it was there. It was just an Al Clapp "thing." After he left us, he claimed some other career landmarks, among them ramrodding an international conference on housing, helping to establish Granville Island and its popular farmers' market, and convincing the provincial government to light up the Lions Gate Bridge as part of the Expo 86 celebrations.

I had heard of Cameron Bell long before I decided to leave Toronto and come to the West Coast. They were not flattering descriptions so I arrived at BCTV expecting to meet an overbearing boor of a man with an overblown sense of his own importance. He was none of that. He was anxious from the outset to establish a rapport with my little CTV bureau and, I guess because I had Toronto experience, prove to me that the East was not, as most people who worked there were convinced, the "centre of the universe." We got along fine. I didn't mind contributing to his daily news show after I'd sent my day's work down the line to Toronto. He would use my stories as they were or break them down to suit the show's purposes. The arrangement worked well for both of us, inasmuch as I was known for some of the offbeat stories I preferred to cover, and I could leave to his people the day-to-day stuff, which I in turn could shuffle off to the CTV national news. Cameron and I became friends. We partied together, skied at Whistler with other friends and later shared a disdain for the creators of the national news.

To him there were no bounds when it came to telling stories on television. His reporters were taught to write to the edited version of their stories on film, rather than have an editor cut their film to the script. The system worked as did so many of his other innovations. He always fought for new technology. His input into the annual capital budget always revolved around the cutting-edge equipment that he believed would help keep us ahead of the competition, with the result that we were among the first organizations in Canada to switch from film to tape cameras. When the *News Hour* became a ratings success, Cameron's star rose along with the audience numbers, especially back East where he had been judged a maverick who railed against the traditional ways of news gathering and presentation.

As I recall, Cameron had been the first anchor on the *News Hour*, having been recruited from local radio where he'd been, among other things, a traffic reporter covering Vancouver. His claim to fame was an on-air car crash between his own and another vehicle just as he was warning his listeners of the dangers of rush-hour driving that morning. While his driving may have been suspect, he excelled at television, especially news coverage. Because he had been an anchor, we shared some very definite ideas about my role in the program. He would coax and cajole me—very much like a film director—to give it my best. I owe him a huge debt. To those of us who knew and worked with him, as ornery as he could get sometimes, he was something of a god. You may not have liked him but you sure as hell had respect for him.

That was also true, though in a much more grudging way, of Keith Bradbury, Cameron's second-in-command. When I arrived in Vancouver to take over the CTV bureau, he was a feature reporter for the *News Hour* and he was allotted, on a frequent basis, his own block of time within the newscast to present his takes on whatever issue he thought was worthy. (Whenever Bradbury didn't fill his time slot, it went to Helen Slinger who had a strong following of her own and a unique style and management skills that she eventually took to the CBC.) At first I couldn't figure Keith out. He had none of the outward finesse of a reporter, but he had such an air of authority about him, such an earnest delivery, that his listeners were drawn into what he had to say. I suddenly realized why this was after I discovered that he had taken his law degree at UBC, and during his years of study there he had also been the editor-in-chief of the well-respected university paper, the *Ubyssey*. After that he had put in some time at the *Vancouver Sun* as a copy editor. Perhaps it had been those experiences that pushed him in our direction instead of into some lucrative Vancouver law practice.

Although Keith was good at reporting, he was even better as an assignment editor. He sensed a story where no one else did or could, or he would suggest a "sidebar" that nobody else could come up with. And he drove his reporters relentlessly—a little too relentlessly, I thought—but you couldn't deny he got results. If you were on the reporting staff, you lived in fear that at the end of your shift you might be called into Keith's office to explain why your story flopped that day, why the ingredients he expected were not there, or why a fact unearthed by a competing reporter on another TV station hadn't been included in your version of the story. Nothing, he felt, should ever elude you. For a while at the end of Cameron Bell's reign after I had become a vice-president of news and public affairs, I was Keith's boss, and I fielded dozens of complaints from reporters who felt they were being put upon by him. I took their complaints to his office but his only observation was "They're just a bunch of weenies." I could only observe that his constant hammering at them made them better reporters in the long run. After Keith retired to the Sunshine Coast, he kept his hand in by becoming consultant to all of Global's news operations across the country. I hope they took his expertise to heart.

Oddly enough it was at Keith's home near Sechelt one sunny summer afternoon that he, Bell, Peters and I got together for lunch to discuss the idea of collaborating on a book about the *News Hour* and its evolution as one of the highest-rated local news programs in North America. In its heyday it out-rated all but a couple of similar shows on the continent. (One of them was in New York City.) We often took advantage of the bragging rights that went with that accomplishment and always worked to keep it in the top ten. That lunch was lighthearted and thoroughly enjoyable. We reminisced about some of the great moments we had shared as the program was groomed to its winning status. But for some reason we left Keith's home without agreeing on the book idea, and I can't recall it being mentioned again. I still think it would have been a winner. All three had been part of the process long before I came along and could have added so much to the telling. Sadly Keith died about a year later, long before his time but leaving behind an admirable legacy.

Of course, without its reporters, producers, editors, researchers and the like, the *News Hour*'s popularity might have been diminished considerably. I think of the talents of John Daly; of Harvey Oberfield, a force to be reckoned with during his days as our Ottawa correspondent; of Clem Chapple, whose no-nonsense approach to running our bureau at the legislature in Victoria always kept us ahead of the pack; of Clive Jackson, a keen assignment editor; of Brian Coxford, a reporter who has a service record longer than my own with the *News Hour*; and of Ted Chernicki, Mike McCardell and Linda Aylesworth. The list also includes some comparative newcomers such as Ted Field, Ron Benze, Aaron McArthur and Grace Ke. There are still reporters on staff today who were at the *News Hour* before I arrived, and I have always said this fact is one of the key reasons for our enduring popularity: viewers are much more comfortable with faces they know, people they have come to trust.

The "on-air talent" has invariably shaped the success of the show as well, and my more than three decades as a member of that group are matched by other very distinguished performers. My first partners were the established weather personality Norm Grohmann, who had a phenomenal following, and sports personality Bernie Pascall, a Prairie boy with whom I had worked at CFTO in Toronto. Norm broke into radio in Chilliwack in 1954 and came to BCTV in 1970 for a nine-year stint to be followed by another run from 1983 to 1998. I always felt a bit wary of Norm. His weather schtick was humour-based, and I sensed that he deemed that to be his domain alone between six and seven every evening, and any attempt at a joke or a little lightness by another cast member absolutely rubbed him the wrong way. We soon recognized that some topics were sacrosanct and we stayed away from them. He was especially known for his Halloween antics, and every year, aided by makeup and costumes (often a dress), he created some insane character to deliver the weather, and I'm sure our viewers were rolling off their couches. Some of his characters were hilarious, such as Byron Something-or-Other, who sported dreadlocks and delivered the forecast with a Jamaican accent. Others were merely funny. But they all scored big with the audience. Who can take exception to success? I still think of him as among "the noted" in terms of broadcast talent.

I played the occasional golf game with Norm, and although avid about the game, he had an aggravating habit of holding up play whenever he came across a hole with a water hazard. That's when he went fishing for errant golf balls. His ball retriever was always at hand to replenish his ball supply even if it drove everyone else to distraction. Sometimes Norm was lovable, sometimes not. Still, he always seemed to be concerned about others around him and would willingly spend time listening to stories of real or imagined problems on the show or off. He's also a survivor, having conquered prostate cancer, and continues to this day as a spokesman for cancer-fighting causes.

Norm is an actor, too, having scored as Felix in the Vancouver Arts Club's production of Neil Simon's *The Odd Couple* and garnering further acclaim as Fagin in the Royal City Musical Theatre's version of *Oliver*. And back in 1970 he joined the cast of the CBC's *Dr. Bundolo's Pandemonium Medicine Show* where he worked with another equally talented guy named Bill Reiter. It was Bill who taught me a little about stage presence when we shared the stage in a charity production of *A Funny Thing Happened on the Way to the Forum*. It had a two-night run in North Vancouver where it raised a few thousand dollars but very little praise from the critics. I had suggested the idea based on my early experience with that British oddity, the pantomime. Every Christmas during school holidays, my mother, aunt or uncle had herded us to London's West End to see some male radio or film star, usually dressed in drag, indulge in unbelievable silliness as the lead in productions like *Jack and the Beanstalk* or *Cinderella*. It was something we looked forward to, though looking back, I can't imagine why. The concept has been tried in other countries but it only draws an audience in England. My idea for a fundraiser was to do something of the same nature but without the female impersonation; it required hours of rehearsal after work, but it turned out to be fun and in a way a learning experience as my comfort level in front of an audience improved. I haven't tried acting since, though some people would claim that what I do on a nightly basis is well within the realm of acting.

In 1979 when Norm Grohmann decided he'd had enough of the *News Hour* for a while, we asked Fred Latremouille to move from the CBC into our weather slot. However, while he was and is a terrific performer, and as much as I liked him and enjoyed working alongside him, I never felt he was totally sold on the idea. I sensed that being the weatherman on television was just something he would do until another opportunity came along. After a couple of years he ran up against management over contract renewals and details and returned to radio, which was truly his medium. He excelled at it, running up very high ratings on a morning show he fronted with his wife Cathy Baldazzi. Then in 2000 they tired of the early hours and the rigours of daily broadcasting and opted for a better lifestyle, sharing their time between homes on the Lower Mainland and Hawaii. They staged a comeback in 2006, hammering out what I thought was the perfect arrangement in the form of a four-day week, working out of their home. That lasted for a year then they were gone again. No one knows, except the two of them, what circumstances led to their final decision, but I hope they're truly happy away from broadcasting. But then you never know when Fred will pop up again.

Politics in British Columbia

MY INTRODUCTION TO THE GOINGS-ON in the legislature in Victoria was an introduction to then-Premier Dave Barrett. And if politics in this part of the world has always had more than a slight touch of the frontier about it, there's no doubt he was the gunslinger on that frontier, though a very likeable guy as far as I was concerned. He was no slouch at oration either and could bring an audience, partisan or otherwise, to cheers and laughter.

Barrett had been a social worker and a civil servant at a time when government employees were not allowed to run for public office. That didn't stop him. He fought for the right to run in the 1960 election and won the Dewdney seat for the provincial CCF party. Subsequently, he ran for the leadership of the party, by then called the New Democrats, but lost to Tom Berger; after Berger lost the 1969 election, one that the NDP expected to win, Barrett was drafted to lead the party. What Berger couldn't do Barrett managed, knocking off W.A.C. Bennett and his Socred government in September 1972. Barrett had an impressive list of accomplishments in office, including reformation of the welfare system in British Columbia and establishment of a Labour Relations Board, the Agricultural Land Reserve and the not-always-popular Insurance Corporation, the auto insurance arm of government. But I still think people looked on him as something of a political buffoon. He had little to back up his ambitions when he launched his career in politics—at least not in the conventional sense. He was neither a lawyer nor a rich man, just a neophyte with good intentions.

After three years of Barrett's reforms, however, W.A.C. had his revenge when his son Bill sent Barrett sprawling in the electoral dust, a victim of his own decision to call a snap election. Even his own constituents turned their backs on him, but he was returned to the legislature in a by-election the following year as the MLA for Vancouver East and led the NDP in the elections of 1979 and 1983. Barrett went to Ottawa in 1988, beginning a stint on the national stage as the member for a Vancouver Island riding, Esquimalt–Juan de Fuca. I always thought he was a misfit in that rarefied atmosphere, and in 1993 when he backed away from party policy on the Meech Lake and Charlottetown accords and voiced his concern over Western alienation, he seemed to prove that theory. He pretty much watched from the political sidelines after that, offering opinions now and then and serving as an analyst on our CTV coverage of election returns. He was good at that and, to say the least, entertaining.

From a journalist's point of view, I think that Barrett

made politics really interesting. I enjoyed covering him, though I was never sure whether it was an act, part of his perceived buffoonery. Sometimes it seemed like a game— one he dearly relished—but whatever it was, he was usually good for a couple of stories a week. However, on a number of occasions my stuff on BC's politics was relegated to the farthest end of the nightly newscast on CTV partly, I think, because my editors couldn't believe that such insanity was rife in Canadian politics. They'd say, "C'mon, that really didn't happen, did it?" And then probably expecting that the rest of country wouldn't believe it either, they down-played it. Alex Macdonald, the attorney general of the day, an avid tennis player and a man I liked immensely, pretty well summed it up for me during a cable program on which we both appeared. He looked down the table at me during a discussion of some issue of the day and said, "You guys from the East must be shaking your heads over what happens out here on the West Coast. It's not like hanging out with the Big Blue Machine, is it?" That, of course, was a reference to the Bill Davis Tories, who were, by comparison to Alex and his cohorts, much more standoffish with reporters. In fact, where the media was concerned, no one could ever say that the Big Blue Machine didn't control the provincial agenda.

But Barrett's relations with the media were not always smooth; on one occasion he trod heavily on the protocol of the day by confronting a prominent journalist in a very public fashion. Marjorie Nichols covered the Victoria scene for the *Vancouver Sun* and covered it aggressively, and along with her colleagues Jim Hume, Alan Garr and Jack

Webster, she dogged Barrett from the very beginning of his tenure. Not to say that he wasn't an easy target, given his flamboyance and the controversy that surrounded almost his every move. But Marjorie, whom I admired much more than Barrett, hit on a particular nerve when she quoted him in one of her columns and he denied having said it. The premier then went in for the kill, confronting her in the halls of the legislature in front of a lot of other reporters, thereby changing the rules of politician/journalist intercourse. Until that time I think that politicians were more afraid of journalists because certain among them, including Marjorie Nichols, had a lot of power. I know that a lot of politicians hated coming to talk to Jack Webster because they knew he would get them into a corner. Journalists were simply more powerful then.

But Marjorie's set-to with Barrett signalled a defining moment in provincial politics, the moment when fear of journalists dissipated in the offices of the premier and his colleagues. After that, it became more difficult for us to go after them, though that didn't mean that we backed away. We still went after them with a vengeance when anything happened in Victoria that we thought was circumspect. It wasn't a matter of setting an agenda; it was just going after them and putting their feet to the fire. We still do that. But I think there are certain politicians who think that the media isn't biting as hard as they used to. Many of them will call a reporter into their offices and say, "Can we talk about this? Either you are mistaken or I am, so let's work this out. If I'm right, I want you to publish a retraction, and if I'm wrong, let's accept that fact."

At the same time I have to say that the media is very, very careful about possible libel today. Perhaps lawyers weren't such a big part of this business when I came to BCTV as they are today. Early in the game we would take a flyer on a lot more things than we do now, so there are fewer libel cases than there were then. I've been named in several lawsuits—that is, I've been sued as part and parcel of a lawsuit because, as a matter of law, I was the messenger, the words came out of my mouth—but I've never been sued successfully.

As for the Barrett/Nichols encounter, elsewhere in the country it might have provoked outrage. For British Columbians it was just another day in the life of the legislature and, besides, the rest of us knew that Marjorie could hold her own against the toughest adversary—premier or otherwise. (Sadly, she died of smoking-related cancer in 1991 when she was only forty-eight years old. A terrible loss for journalism as it should always have been practised.)

As a reporter and later as the anchor for the *News Hour*, I had several approaches from incumbent administrations, trying to get me "on side." One came via Pam Glass from Kim Campbell during her short-lived stint as prime minister. Pam was only doing her job, I suppose, when she suggested I might enjoy a lunch with the prime minister, who had some serious concerns about our ongoing coverage of her policies. Instead of politely declining, I agreed to meet the PM at the Bayshore Inn. I listened politely as we both munched our salads or whatever, was flattered that she thought it was all up to me, lingered over coffee then, as she paid the tab, thanked her and left. As I walked through the hotel lobby I forgot—rather impolitely, I suppose—every word of our conversation and went back to the newsroom to carry on my day. I never mentioned it to anyone else in our operation.

Mike Harcourt, the premier of BC from 1991 to 1996, had one of his aides arrange a game of golf with me at Shaughnessy, my home course, so Harcourt, I felt later, could convince me to be a bit more benevolent in our coverage of his government. In a way I was again flattered that the perception seemed to be that I ran everything in the newsroom at BCTV but not so flattered that I would even entertain the idea of being, as I guess they wanted, a mouthpiece for the government of the day. I always thought that, as over-critical as we may have seemed, we were ultimately fair. I don't remember our scores that day, but I'm pretty sure he didn't beat me. I am sure he left without getting what he wanted.

All of this might prompt a discussion about the wisdom of reporters becoming overly chummy with politicians, especially when it comes to the government in Victoria. It's a danger at the best of times, but trying to exist together at arm's length in an isolated situation such as that presented by the West Coast is difficult, to say the least. Most of this province's politicians and the reporters who cover their activities come from other parts of the province so probably share the same need for some kind of common comfort found in camaraderie—as well as drinks at the Bengal Lounge in the old Empress Hotel. I always thought that

Andy Stephen, our legislative correspondent back in the '70s and '80s, came close to crossing the line. A big man, reputedly a musician (as in singer of songs) and gregarious to a fault, Andy was my main contact whenever I crossed over to Victoria to cover a story for the CTV *National*. We always met in the press gallery for a briefing, I would file my story, and inevitably we wound up at some local bar, and whether by Andy's design or not, some local MLA or even a cabinet minister would share the evening with us. It wasn't difficult to figure out that this was Andy's routine, and I made a mental note to warn him that the perception, at least, was dangerous. Not that Andy ever made a secret of his friendships, often boasting of visiting with Premier W.A.C. Bennett at Bennett's home or being on close terms with Emery Barnes or some other MLA. I can't recall any of his reports that smacked of "inside information," but I often wondered if he'd been over there in Victoria far too long. There is a very big difference, I should say, between "contacts" and friends. In this business you should have contacts. You must be wary of friendships.

I'm reminded of another discussion involving Jack Webster and others about journalists becoming members of government, usually at the end of a career in broadcast journalism or newspapers. Jack said—and I agree—"How can any honest journalist, having spent his life criticizing these people [politicians], suddenly become one of them?" I wonder what Jack would think about the makeup of today's Senate, which includes Mike Duffy and Pamela Wallin. Duffy, especially, made his mark poking and prodding the government of the day, both with good humour and without, in the most important way. I have always had a great admiration for him and his ways, but I'm not sure about his place in that great chamber of sober second thought. We'll have to wait and see. (For the record, I haven't been asked to put my name up for possible inclusion on the government back benches. It's just not something that interests me.)

Bill Vander Zalm only complained openly to me on one occasion, making it clear he definitely didn't like the way we characterized his comings and goings. He was in our studio for an interview on Jack Webster's morning talk show, and afterward he sought out Clem Chapple, our legislative correspondent (and one of the best), and myself. "Give me a break" was the message he delivered, wrapping it around the idea that the two of us always gave him short shrift. There's never enough time on a nightly news program for in-depth interviews, but obviously he thought he was owed more than others. I think we were hoping he would just go away if we challenged his complaint, so off the top of our heads we offered him an open-ended interview, no holds barred and with no chance to preview our questions. He accepted. We swallowed hard but we went ahead. As it turned out, there wasn't much in it that our viewers didn't already know, just a rehash of Vander Zalmisms and current government policies. But he went away happy.

Vander Zalm always seemed larger than life to me but I quite liked him and his headband-wearing wife, Lillian. But just a minute here! Is it possible to take seriously a man who created a tempest in the legislature over bilingual cereal boxes, or who once suggested that the answer to all our welfare problems would be to have the jobless and destitute among us pick up shovels and go to work, or who was depicted in a Bob Bierman cartoon in the *Victoria Times* picking the wings off flies (Vander Zalm sued and won in BC Supreme Court but the verdict was reversed by the Court of Appeal), or who fought sex education in schools and tried to cut abortion funding? And did I mention Vander Zalm's money-losing theme-style tourist attraction Fantasy Gardens or the subsequent Faye Leung episode? Leung was the woman who acted as the broker between the Vander Zalms and the eventual buyer of Fantasy Gardens, a Taiwanese businessman named Tan Yu. Night after night for several months this slightly dotty real estate agent provided us with comic relief, however serious her plight might have been. Her ongoing attacks on Bill and Lillian concerned alleged non-payment of her commission, but what assigned her to provincial history was her array of hats. She must have had an enviable wardrobe because her every appearance featured a different style and colour of headgear. Somehow—despite her and all the other obstacles—Vander Zalm managed to survive the onslaught into a second term. In his autobiography his assessment of those days is set in less than glowing terms. Looking back and contemplating his forced resignation after being charged with "criminal breach of trust" (of which he was subsequently cleared) and influence-peddling while in office, he quotes himself in a conversation with his lawyer friend Mel Smith: "I've grown tired of this phoney business where forthrightness, openness and honesty are a disadvantage." Excuse me?

In retrospect, I think the days of Bill Bennett's leadership had a certain "ivory tower" feel to them. He and his family were moneyed and secure in their lives, much more so than their grassroots constituents, and this circumstance promoted an aloofness that was palpable. He was not known as gregarious, even among his legislative colleagues, but given his father's popularity and political clout, perhaps he was keeping himself focussed on success in order to prove his own capabilities. Bennett had an admirable list of accomplishments, not the least of which was Expo 86, heavily promoted by the Socreds and mounted despite all manner of opposition, including an anti-Expo stance by then-mayor of Vancouver Mike Harcourt, who would himself become premier in 1991. History will also record Bennett's hassles with labour unions in the province. Until they ran headlong into Socred policy, they had pretty much written their own agenda in BC, so the clashes led to a bitter general strike in 1983 that would feature an angry crowd of sixty thousand union sympathizers marching in protest, waving their placards and shouting their anti-Bennett slogans as they went.

I have always said that being in politics breeds arrogance, but I also believe it breeds insecurity. That was brought home to me one night during an annual benefit dinner staged by the Greek community in Vancouver. My table mate on that occasion was Jim Nielsen, a former radio talk-show host on CJOR who had moved into politics and become health minister in Bill Bennett's cabinet. During the meal he leaned over to me and said in an accusatory way, "Why do you always shoot the premier with a fish-eye lens?" I was taken aback, to say the least. In the first place, to my knowledge no camera we ever used featured a fish-eye lens, the kind that rounds out an image so that it has the contours of a blowfish. In the second place, why, even if we could, would we do it? But the minister left the table convinced that we were using technology to undermine his premier and his party. It seemed to me odd that this man, as knowledgeable as he should have been about the media, would make such an accusation. And I wondered how his boss felt about it.

Glen Clark made his way onto the provincial stage in 1996. He is, as most of his fans and backers would tell you, "the salt of the earth," perhaps because he is a product of blue-collar East Vancouver, and before he became an MLA, he had been an organizer for the Ironworkers Union. He was handed the finance portfolio in the Harcourt cabinet and went on to replace his boss when Harcourt stepped down. Then, against all odds, he led his party to an election victory in 1996. His fortunes seemed to be on the rise until a neighbour, a building contractor named Dimitros Pilarinos who had applied for a gambling licence, did some renovations on the premier's modest home on Anzio Drive in Burnaby. What happened next is part of the sometimes unbelievable political history of this province. Around seven on the evening of March 2, 1999, RCMP officers raided the premier's home to look for evidence that the premier had used his influence to get Pilarinos a charity casino licence. Clark was subsequently charged with one count of breach of trust and another of accepting a benefit, and he resigned on August 25, 1999. Three years later after a 136-day trial, he was acquitted of all charges. BC Supreme Court Justice Elizabeth Bennett ruled that "there is no question Mr. Clark exercised poor judgment in hiring Mr. Pilarinos to do renovations for him when Mr. Pilarinos had an application for a casino licence before the government. However, there is nothing in his conduct that crosses the line from an act of folly to behaviour calling for criminal sanctions." Glen Clark had meanwhile taken a job in the corporate world created by Jimmy Pattison, where he remains happily today.

On the night of the raid on the Clark residence BCTV managed to score an exclusive on the story, and by doing so we became part of the story ourselves. John Daly, our go-to guy when it comes to crime and punishment issues, had received information about the impending RCMP operation and, after scouting out the area, arrived at the Clark home with cameras rolling. Raw footage of the whole thing appeared on the *News Hour* within minutes of the raid. How, the competition probably wondered as I'm sure NDP supporters did, had Daly managed to be the only reporter on the scene? I must admit I wondered myself. But I knew John had strong contacts with almost every police force on the Lower Mainland and they trusted him. Of course, the New Democrats smelled a rat, suggesting that we were tipped off by Liberal Party supporters who had instigated the whole thing themselves. After the story had been regurgitated time and time again in the next few months,

I became a little fed up with the accusations against Daly and the *News Hour* and by association myself as well, so I went directly to our news director, Keith Bradbury, and demanded to know if we'd violated any journalistic codes in our coverage. No, I was assured, we didn't. I went to air that night, leaned into the camera lens and told our viewers just that. No jiggery-pokery, no sleight of hand, no way, no how. We had simply done our job. I don't know how effective this was, but I felt better. I did feel a twinge of sympathy for Mr. Clark. But now he has carved himself a niche in the corporate world and in all likelihood doesn't miss the heat of the spotlight in Victoria one bit.

Dan Miller, who had been deputy premier during Clark's term as head of government, served as interim premier pending a leadership vote that brought Ujjal Dosanjh to the job. Then the Gordon Campbell Liberals swept into office where they are now firmly entrenched. Before he came to Victoria, I had only known Mr. Campbell in a passing sense. I knew who he was, he knew who I was, and that went back to his days at Vancouver City Hall. Even then, I recall, he had the lean and hungry look of an aspiring politician, eager for power but content to wait for that opportune moment, happy to deal with the issues that confronted him on a municipal basis, knowing that he wasn't just spinning his tires. If there's one word I would use to describe him it would be "shrewd," but even he, in a province that seems to have the patent on political scandal, has stumbled. His enemies, and the media, indulged in a feeding frenzy when one night in January 2003 he was arrested in Hawaii for driving under the influence after leaving a party. A breathalyzer test revealed he was trying to negotiate a Maui highway with twice the legal amount of alcohol in his system. He consequently (and probably wisely) hurried back to BC to make a public apology and to vow never to drink again. Who knows? But the incident did not seem to damage his image or his popularity beyond redemption. That may not be the case with the fallout from the RCMP raid on the legislature in December 2003 and the resultant court case involving breach of trust in the sale of BC Rail. These events, along with the introduction of the dreaded harmonized sales tax (HST), could spell the end of the current Liberal administration in the next election.

Funny thing about this province from a journalist's point of view—and I'm sure it applies elsewhere—is viewer perception. Be critical of a party and its policies and you are branded anti-NDP, anti-Socred, anti-Liberal or whatever. Point out a strong point—in new legislation, for instance— and suggest it might serve the common good, and you are suddenly—yesterday's story notwithstanding—pro-NDP, pro-Socred, pro-Liberal or whatever. It all depends, as they say, on whose ox is being gored, but it's frustrating as hell for anyone in this business.

My Italian roots. My maternal grandfather emigrated from Italy to England before World War I to join other relatives who owned a gelato business in the west end of London.

My parents, John and Julie, on their wedding day. Julie Parsonage was a tiny woman with a beatific face who lived for her kids, while John Parsonage was a sombre disciplinarian and my siblings and I did not miss him much during his frequent absences.

e I am as a grumpy toddler with older ers Anne on my left, and Phyllis on my right. 1 though we didn't have much money our her always ensured that there was food on table and that we were dressed neatly.

My mother, grandfather and me during the war years in London.

My sister Diane and I pose for a photo a few years before moving to Canada.

Here I am with three of my sisters on an outing to Wasaga Beach on Lake Huron. That's Anne in the hat standing next to Phyllis, and Diane is sitting next to me.

Grade nine at St. Jerome's College in Kitchener, Ontario, 1953. I'm seated in the centre, fifth from right.

I am in my early radio days, ~ring to an audience of farmers, ~sewives and people who tuned in ~d out who had died over the last ~le of days—the perfect training ~ long career in broadcasting.

After trying out Feversham and Kitchener, eventually the Parsonage family ended up in Sarnia, Ontario, of all places. Here's a rare photo of all the Parsonage siblings together, mid '50s. Right to left: Kathy, Diane, me, Phyllis, Anne and big brother John.

~rfect score: an enthusiastic judge for this ~t in the 1970s.

Touted by the *Burnaby Times* as "The Man of the News Hour," 1979.

On the set of the *News Hour* with Bernie Pascal.

While many politicians feared Jack Webster and his critical approach, I greatly respected him.

In the early days at BCTV.

Garnering respect and renown as a youthful newscaster in the 1980s (*Vancouver Magazine*, August 1983).

...e opening of Wibbler's restaurant in ...ouver with BCTV producer Lawrence Donald.

The first promotional ad for the *News Hour* on BCTV.

The six o'clock stars in 1983, left to right: Joanna Piros, Pamela Martin, Bill Good, me, Wayne Cox, Cecilia Walters, Len Grant and Doriana Temolo.

Benefit hockey game, January 1987. I'm in the back row, at left.

"We love Squire Barnes." Squire almost didn't get hired by Ron Bremner, but he became a favourite of viewers.

Fred Latremouille is a great performer and I enjoyed working with him at the *News Hour*. He and his wife, Cathy Baldazzi, make a terrific team, both on and off the air.

Sorting out last-minute changes with set producer Steve Wyatt and Pamela Martin.

economic downturn of the y '90s forced me to cut staff at *News Hour*, giving the *Sun* the ortunity to rather unfairly term me Slasher."

Helping out the food bank with Jennifer Mather (now Burke).

The Variety Club Telethon (here with Jill Krop, Wayne Cox and the ever-present Charlie) is a worthwhile cause that I enjoy supporting every year.

Teeing up. Golf is one of my favourite pastimes.

Travel editor Alec Burden and I sit at the newroom desk, with loyal Charlie in his favourite spot at my feet.

ting some of the *News Hour* fans in Fernie, BC.

nagan Wine Festival judges holding each other up, left to right: Park Heffelfinger, Coke Roth, Mark Filatow, Barbara Philip, Sara D'Amato, Jay Drysdale and Tim Pawsey.

Charlie, a very special cocker spaniel, came into my life looking for a home and found his way into my heart.

Charlie was a beloved presence in the newsroom and, not surprisingly, garnered a large fan base over time.

Charlie getting the paparazzi treatment: fans crowd around the car hoping for a glimpse of the furry, four-legged TV star.

Jack steals the spotlight, as usual, as I receive my honorary doctorate from the British Columbia Institute of Technology (BCIT). Behind us are, left to right: Don Wright, President of BCIT; Dawna Mackay, Acting Registrar; and Val Karpinsky, Vice President Student Services.

Tammy looking gorgeous as usual on our wedding day.

I appreciated receiving the Bruce Hutchison Lifetime Achievement Award in 2004, presented by Ian Hanomansing, in recognition of all I have accomplished in my career thus far. DAVE THOMSON PHOTOGRAPHY & DESIGN

At home with my wonderful wife, Tammy.

Ken Soble of Maple Leaf Radio Company owned Hamilton's CHML, where I started as a radio DJ and came into my own as an on-air personality. COURTESY OF CANADIAN ASSOCIATION OF BROADCASTERS

Ray Peters' long and distinguished broadcasting career spanned five decades and culminated with his retirement at the top as CEO of Western International Communications. COURTESY OF RAY AND HEIDI PETERS

One of my first mentors, Harvey Kirck, was a big lovable bear of a guy and we became good friends over the years. COURTESY OF CANADIAN ASSOCIATION OF BROADCASTERS

Ron Bremner's management style was highly motivational but still somewhat tongue-in-cheek. COURTESY OF CANADIAN ASSOCIATION OF BROADCASTERS

I've had the opportunity to witness Trina McQueen's meteoric rise over the years, from her beginnings in 1967 as the first female on-camera reporter for CBC's The National to her retirement in 2003, stepping out at the top as the Chief Operating Officer of CTV. COURTESY OF CANADIAN ASSOCIATION OF BROADCASTERS

Directing the News

ALTHOUGH ART JONES' VANTEL BROADCASTING had won the initial Channel 8 licence for BCTV back in 1960, within two years he sold his shares, and local entrepreneur Frank Griffiths began buying into the company. By 1982 Griffiths' Western International Communications (WIC) had gained control, Ray Peters had become CEO of WIC and Don Smith took over as president of BCTV. During the decade that followed, the news staff grew from six to eighty-six, and the six o'clock *News Hour* became Canada's most-watched local newscast with an audience of 640,000 viewers.

In 1989 WIC became the sole owner of BCTV, and that was also the year that I was promoted to BCTV news director, though I continued to host the *Early News* and the *News Hour*. Four years later we introduced a week-day national newscast called *Canada Tonight*, and I began anchoring a version of it that we recorded at 3:30 in the afternoon so that we could cycle it across the country to other stations, though it was only really successful here and in Alberta. Bill Good was hired to do the local 5:30 version of the show.

I became BCTV's vice-president with responsibility for news and public affairs in 1995. I had complained to Don Smith, who had succeeded Ray Peters in 1982 as president of the company, that the newsroom had no representation in the boardroom, and for some reason—and not because I was wonderfully persuasive—he took my complaint to heart, and I got new business cards. The new job kept me more desk-bound, though I still kept my anchor duties. For a while it also meant a longer day because of the early morning management meetings of the cheerleading variety led by Ron Bremner, who had taken over Don Smith's former spot as general manager and CEO. Bremner was a devoted student of the Stephen Covey school of management and a former CKNW Radio executive. He had, many years earlier, worked for CHML Radio in Hamilton, Ontario, his hometown and one of the stops on my own early career journey. I could see the resemblance in style when he mentioned that one of his mentors was Tom Darling, the station manager who had ultimately been responsible for my move from music to news at that station. The only difference I could see between the two was the amount of bluster they emitted. Darling was much more an explosion waiting to happen, while I always thought that Bremner leaned heavily on a more tongue-in-cheek approach.

I have been very fortunate over the years on the *Early News*, the *News Hour* and *Canada Tonight* to have on-air partners who were like members of my family. From my years of sharing the anchor desk with Pamela Martin to nights with Squire Barnes, Deb Hope and Wayne Cox, I could not have asked for better company. Pamela was always the absolute darling of viewers. A transplanted American and a former "Miss Teen America," she came to BC with her husband who, I'm told, was intent on avoiding the draft in the United States. If I have the story right, she first spoke with news director Cameron Bell about a job in 1975, but he looked at her rather thin resume and suggested she come back after getting experience with some other TV station. Then, he said, he'd consider finding her a place. I don't know whether he thought that would be the end of it, but with typical spunk Pamela went knocking on the door of our sister-station CHEK in Victoria, and they didn't hesitate. She began her career with them by co-hosting and producing *Daybreak* then spent a year at CKNW as that radio station's first female beat reporter. Not long after, with her on-air skills sharpened and her experience with interviews and news stories newly honed, she went back to Bell to remind him of his promise. And he kept it. She stayed with BCTV until 2001 when it became a member station of the Global Network.

By then CTV had shifted its affiliation to a new station on Burrard Street in downtown Vancouver, and station boss Bob Hurst was looking for personnel to front its news operation. Hurst had come up through the ranks; we had been reporters together at CFTO before Hurst, at age twenty-six, became news director there, having reaped a number of prestigious awards for his reporting. Now Hurst came to me, expecting I could be lured to CTV's side. It was tempting. At a meeting in a suite provided by the network in a downtown hotel that was just a walk away from his office, he began his pitch by allowing that "we know how much money you make and that doesn't scare us." Then he added that he thought it might be a good idea if they flew me to Toronto for an interview with Trina McQueen, his boss, who had also been a colleague of mine in those days around the CFTO desk in the *Telegram* building. Trina had a meteoric rise from there. She went from being the first female reporter for CFTO then the first female co-host of *W5* to becoming in 1967 the first on-camera reporter for the CBC's *The National*. She was at the helm for the CBC's launch of *Newsworld* and then masterminded the launch of the Canadian Discovery Channel. In 2000 she became president and chief operating officer of the CTV Network. (She retired in 2003.)

But getting acquainted with Trina again was not in my plans. I admit I was being a bit mischievous in this affair. I really just wanted to have a look at the planning side of this new operation, our new competition, and so I went along with the possibility of my shifting alliances until the moment I left the hotel that day. I went straight back to my office and wrote a letter to Hurst saying thanks for the offer but I preferred to stay where I was. Besides, I told him, I had some time left in my present contract and thought it would be disloyal and dishonest to walk out on BCTV.

Hurst had better luck with Pamela. It's tough for anyone

to go on playing "anchor-in-waiting" when you have your heart set on being the prime six o'clock anchor in a work situation that you like. If I had accepted Hurst's offer, she would have been provided with her rightful place in succession, but she knew I was not about to leave. And that, I suspect, was the principal factor in Pamela's decision. She accepted an offer from CTV. And I'm guessing the money CTV was offering was far and above the salary she commanded with us.

But there was, I thought, a certain irony attached to her leaving. Just before she made the decision to accept the CTV offer, we got word that *Canada Tonight*, which went to air at five thirty every night, would be cancelled to make way for a Global version of the national news read by Kevin Newman, a Canadian broadcaster with experience at the American network ABC. This shift would mean that Bill Good, who had been reading *Canada Tonight* after putting in an arduous shift as a talk-show host and news reader on CKNW, would have no show. To make up for this loss, our strategy would be to slot him in as co-anchor on the five o'clock news, sharing that thirty minutes with Pamela. But when this became known, a bomb went off. Pamela was outraged. It was, she railed, a form of punishment, and what had she done to deserve such treatment after working so hard for ratings? Why, she demanded, was she being saddled with a co-anchor? And then she resigned. It might have been only a few days later that Bill, facing contract negotiations with us and uncertain about staying on at BCTV if it meant becoming an unwelcome addition to

Pamela's program, accepted an offer from CTV to—yes, as fate would have it—co-anchor with Pamela Martin at six.

We can only imagine what Pamela thought about this development because she accepted Bill's coming on board without public comment. To this day they still seem uncomfortable with each other on air. And perhaps off. Whatever the case, at this writing, they have yet to defeat us as the ratings leader in this market. Having said that, their product is not to be sneered at. They have a talented pool of reporters behind them, and their content is, in my opinion, right up there with ours. If they survive the economic storms that have been raging in this country lately, and there's no reason to think they won't, someday they may be more successful than we are. Still, it's very difficult for any new station, in any market, to knock off the established leader because it's a function of familiarity and longevity. Viewers cling to the comfort of familiar faces. Being a newcomer means you first have to create the product and then nurture it until it becomes noticeable and, in the long run, credible when stacked up against the current favourite. Not easy to do as a look at any Toronto station will confirm. For years CFTO, the giant CTV affiliate, has been the target of newer news operations whose avowed aim has been to knock them off in the ratings wars. But it's never happened despite the fact, or perhaps because of it, that CFTO's six o'clock broadcast has changed very little in the past three decades. Their news set might have been tweaked once or twice, but the basic presentation has remained unchanged in the years since I left that newsroom and came to Vancouver.

Deborra Hope became Pamela Martin's replacement at

BCTV in 2001, hosting the *Early News* and the "Insight" segment on the *News Hour* at six. Deb has an impressive background as a reporter, having cut her journalistic teeth in the print and wire-service leagues. She is also one of those rare people who was born and raised in this province, her birthplace being Trail, the Interior centre that seems to produce more athletes and broadcasters than any other city in BC. Before she came to BCTV she worked for Canadian Press and United Press International but took no time at all adapting to the television version of journalism. I don't think there's a situation she can't handle, from interviews with some of our top politicians to emcee appearances at charity events. She made a steady rise through the ranks to where she is today, and she's an utter delight to work with. She has a work ethic that is (or should be) the envy of every other reporter—she just doesn't quit. And she's raised a family at the same time.

Three things viewers might not know about Deb—one, she is a former soccer player (she and her team once competed in the Provincial Games); two, she is a talented singer; and three, she has an infectious sense of humour. Deb is one-quarter of an *a capella* quartet known as Over the Moon that has in the past few years won a huge share of prizes at North American Sweet Adeline competitions. For a price Deb and her group will serenade your sweetheart on Valentine's Day at his/her office or home. I really like having Deb as a partner on the *News Hour* because she is an audience in her own right. No matter how bad or how corny the jokes (on and off air) get, you can count on her to deliver the sympathetic reaction—a loud, appreciative laugh that just borders on electrified frenzy.

Squire Barnes' career with us began on a strange note. In 1990 Ron Bremner, a well-respected executive with CKNW Radio, had replaced Don Smith as general manager and CEO at BCTV. A couple of years into his reign in a conversation regarding the state of our sports department, Ron raised Squire's name and said, in effect, that no matter how desperate we got for new blood, Squire Barnes was a no-go under any circumstances. The message was clear: do not hire that guy. Period. I don't recall whether Ron outlined his objections to Squire. Was it looks or was it style? Or was it the name? But okay, you're the boss, Ron! I went back to my office and struck Squire's name off my list of possible candidates for a weekend on-air job. Somehow, though, the word didn't filter down to the weekend producer who had been at CBC around the same time Squire was working there and liked his work. So much so that, as the authority for Saturdays and Sundays, he took it upon himself to offer the job to Barnes. And Squire, not knowing a thing about the politics surrounding the affair, accepted. I wasn't about to reverse that decision despite Ron's edict, and so Squire came to work at BCTV. It wasn't long before Bremner appeared in my office, and I expected a thorough chewing out.

"Whose idea was it to hire Squire Barnes?" he asked.

I hesitated a bit and then, anxious to protect myself and the weekend producer, finally blurted, "Why?"

"Because," he said, "it was a damned good idea. The

guy grows on you. Even the viewers like him." Well, at least he admitted his mistake—sort of.

But there is another strange story about Squire Barnes. Before he came to BCTV, he had worked in radio for a few years, specializing in sports, then ended up working at CBC Television, writing and producing for the popular sportscaster Eric Dwyer, who became his friend and mentor. Then oddly enough, after Eric left the corporation, Squire, who was by then our sports director, hired him on a part-time basis. Eric worked a lot of weekends for us then left the business entirely to devote more time to his art (he's a very talented painter) and his golf, a game he's very good at.

When Squire started working full-time for BCTV, his immediate boss was Bernie Pascall, who was already the station's sports director and principal sports anchor when I got to Vancouver in 1974. Bernie and I had worked together at CFTO for a short time and I had lost track of him after he left, so I was happy to see a familiar face. However, I had a problem with Bernie's approach to sports anchoring from the get-go because I thought he was predictable, a sort of cookie-cutter kind of sports personality who would never think of taking on the established sports teams in a critical way. He was also a bit of a "homer" in his approach to local sports. After I shifted to the management role, I called him on this, practically begging him to inject a little journalism into the coverage. His response was simply to ignore me and carry on as usual. No matter what I said, he did it his way, and after a while I simply gave up. At least, I told myself, we had Squire and Barry Houlihan to provide a bit of pizzazz, and I made do with that.

Then came the economic crunch of the late 1990s that sent our accountants downtown into a spate of saving measures: no overtime for reporters, no hiring, no raises, no waste and, by the way, perhaps we should cut staff. I was left to figure out who among the news operation personnel should be cut loose. It was a painful exercise, but I came up with a list of eleven candidates, and that list included Bernie, not because of his refusal to accept my suggestions, but because there were others who could do the job just as well and drag the sports department into new areas. I don't think Bernie ever got over being laid off.

The others I let go that day in 1999 weren't that understanding either, but I didn't expect them to be. Belle Puri, who subsequently went to the CBC, was the most hostile. And Margot Harper, who is now the news director at our CTV opponent, would dearly love revenge in the form of higher ratings for her program, even though her anger is not directed as much toward me as to Keith Bradbury, who handled her actual leaving and with whom she never completely saw eye to eye. However, the whole episode earned me the title of "The Slasher"—at least that was reporter Pete McMartin's way of describing me in the *Vancouver Sun* the following day. I cringed when I saw the description in the cutline under my photo and thought it was a bit unfair, to say the least. I was told later by a staff member that the perception in the newsroom was that we—that is, management—had taken advantage of the downturn in the economy to pare away some underperformers.

An organizing movement had seized the BCTV operation in 1996. The Pulp, Paper and Woodworkers of Canada
polled the staff, and it wasn't long before everyone connected with the newsroom was a card-carrying member of
the PPWC, even the on-air people, who were disappointed
to discover that their inclusion was mandatory. To my way
of thinking, unions don't work that well in broadcasting situations. Until the union was installed at CFTO in
Toronto, we had been a freewheeling group of reporters,
chasing stories all over Ontario at any time of the day or
night. While union regulations may have helped the staff
sort out their grievances with the company, the minute the
union and management negotiated their first agreement,
the atmosphere had definitely changed in the newsroom,
and far too much time was spent on working out real or
perceived differences than on what we were about: news
gathering. After that, no one ever grabbed a cameraperson and raced out the door at the slightest hint of a story.
It all had to be done by the book. And when that book
included restrictions on overtime and compensation for
the extra hours, well-defined meal breaks that, if missed,
meant extra expense for CFTO, and dozens of other rules,
we and our viewers were the worse off for it. It also promoted bad feelings between the full-timers who were union
employees and the freelancing non-union employees who
are such a necessary part of what we do. It just wasn't the
same after that, and it produced a measure of bitterness
that exists to this day.

For the record I was never a member of the union at
BCTV or Global, having achieved the vice-presidency by

the time the union came in. Otherwise, I would have joined my friends and colleagues on the only picket line that ever went up around the building.

Wayne Cox, because he was considered a part-time contract player, was able to stay away from that mess, too, and emerge unscathed. But who could dislike Wayne, anyway? He's like the friendliest neighbour you could ever hope for, the quintessential guy-next-door. Like so many of us, his career began in radio. He started at CKLG-FM in Vancouver before heading to Quesnel in 1968, then to Kamloops and finally back to the coast again in 1971 to do an afternoon drive show, *Wayne Cox and Friends,* for CKNW. He moved to television in 1979 to host the *Vancouver Show* at CKVU and became the weekend weather anchor for the *News Hour* at BCTV in 1997. Along the way he has also hosted a number of syndicated television game shows including *Acting Crazy, Second Honeymoon*, and *Talkabout.* I don't normally find DJs very funny (perhaps because I used to be one) but Wayne was different, as on the day he came back on air after a piece of music and intoned—in his own voice—"This is Demi Moore (or some such female movie star's name), and whenever I'm in Vancouver, I listen to the *Wayne Cox Show.*" It is that kind of humour that carried him through all his years as a game-show host and onto the *News Hour.* He's just fun to be around, especially whenever we took our *News Hour* show "on the road" over the years. For Wayne and a lot of other crew members, going on the road was party time. (Sometime when you see him on the street, ask him to demonstrate his famous "alligator dance." I'm told "it rocks." And I suspect it's fuelled by his uninhibited sense of fun and a fair lashing of a pretty good red wine, which we both enjoy.)

The road shows came about as the result of BCTV launching a new advertising campaign in the mid-1990s in which we branded ourselves as the "TV for BC" station. But only a short time into the campaign we started hearing from viewers across the province that, if we were really "TV for BC," why hadn't we ever mentioned the name of their town or city? And they complained that our weather segments weren't including the forecast for their area. So it was decided that we would take the show to the viewer. Those road trips became the highlights of nearly a decade of the *News Hour* because they gave us a chance to see the province and some places we were unlikely to go otherwise, and they put a face to our audience. They also gave our viewers a better idea of who we were and what we were all about.

Our inauspicious beginning could only be described as local remote, that is, we were away from the news set— but not very far. In fact, we were on Georgia Street near the intersection of Denman where nightly traffic feeds into Stanley Park to go across the Lions Gate Bridge. The only problem was that, by six o'clock when our show goes to air, traffic had dissipated and most folks were already at home in front of their television sets. As a result, it was relatively quiet around me as I said, "Good evening from downtown Vancouver. This is the *News Hour*." In reality it was just me perched on a stool on the back of a rented flatbed truck, protected by canvas windbreaks on three sides. I felt a little embarrassed, wondering what the hell we were doing there, and I suspect most of our critics and some of our viewers wondered the same.

However, it was a beginning. The next year, 1997, we visited Prince George, Quesnel and Williams Lake, and from that trip grew a full-blown television circus that rambled around the province for a week a couple of times a year, doing a town a night. It proved to be wildly popular. In fact, there were times when town officials would openly solicit an appearance by the *News Hour* in their town squares, beachside parks, arenas and downtown malls. Being invited made it so much better and made our province-wide audiences appreciate us even more. The talent loved every moment of it. Pamela Martin and later Deb Hope would spend the hours between programs sorting out the lore of the area and putting together a report for that night's show (though we often joked about Pamela's ability to find a spa wherever we went). Squire, Wayne and I spent most of the day riding fire engines, sightseeing in helicopters and touring hospitals and schools with our local hosts, and we managed to get in a few rounds of golf on some of BC's best courses as well.

I'm sure, if you put it to a vote, that Squire would be rated as the most popular member of our group. People turned up at our broadcast sites armed with huge placards etched with crayon letters singing his praises. And mothers, knowing he was single, brought their daughters to meet the eligible young sports announcer from Vancouver. Nothing ever came of it, but it was fun to watch Squire squirm under the pressure. Next to him, Pamela drew a huge following, as did Deb, and then probably Charlie, my American cocker spaniel, who actually had his own fan club.

But the crew members were the real soldiers of our road show. They worked twelve-hour days and they worked hard. I was amazed at their abilities and proud of them. No matter how much they partied—and they did that with distinction—they never failed to answer the call in the morning, getting the satellite truck and our sets on the road for the next location. By the end of the week, though, they were thoroughly exhausted. On top of that, many of them had to drive back to the Lower Mainland.

We hit every kind of weather, bumped over some challenging roads and highways, almost lost a producer when she wandered into traffic in Trail (thankfully it was just minor cuts and bruises), saw just about every tourist attraction known to man, and met some truly wonderful British Columbians. Whatever it cost—and it wasn't cheap—it was worth it, and we were all sorry when we stopped our tours in 2004 and confined ourselves to the studio with the exception of an occasional foray to Whistler to hype the upcoming Winter Olympic Games. (After CTV acquired the coverage rights to the Games, we were shut out there.) I just hope no other station takes the idea and runs with it. We looked forward to those expeditions and we miss them.

10

My Private and
Not-So-Private Life

PEOPLE WHO KNOW ME might pick up this book just to see how I handle the telling of my personal life, that part outside the studio, away from the lights and the nightly show. To be sure it's a curiosity, sometimes even to me. And at times it's been messy.

Perhaps my old friend Denny Boyd put it best when he remarked on my private life in his response to the cadre of "roasters" who had gathered one evening in 1995 to mark the publication of his last book, *In My Own Words*. I had been asked to simply read a passage from his book. I did my best and was a little jolted when it was Denny's turn to slide behind the podium and, having cut down a couple of other roasters, looked over at me and said to the assembly, "Ah, and then there's Parsons. You can sum up his love life in a single word: NEXT!" It was a little embarrassing though I'm sure he didn't mean it to be, but I winced because it was too close to the truth. My public life in front of the cameras can be, by most measures, described as successful. My private life—and I've tried, with great difficulty, to keep it that way—can be rightly described as a "mess" when it comes to relationships. I can't stack up against Henry the Eighth or Mickey Rooney but I certainly do have exes in my background, and they no doubt would side with Mr. Boyd. I admit that I am sometimes difficult to deal with or to live with.

My first partner and I met at CHML, married quickly and lived to regret it. I think I must have had some kind of Ozzie and Harriet syndrome because I thought we were supposed to marry, have kids and live happily ever after in some vine-covered cottage on a sunny street in "Wherever, Canada." She wanted a husband and a career and couldn't seem to put the two together. It ended in Toronto when I was working the night shift at CHUM.

My second marriage failed because I simply wasn't around much. I had dragged my wife to Vancouver when I took over the West Coast bureau for CTV and from then on spent most of my time away from home searching for stories here, there and everywhere except, it seemed, in Vancouver. My wife soon became bored with her lot in life and tried for a career in television after I settled into the anchor position at BCTV, but her Sunday morning program, directed at the Italian community, lasted only half a season. By then we were leading separate lives. Now she lives in Paris and is the executive marketing director for an events firm she runs with her husband. And she has two beautiful daughters.

My third marriage was to a gracious, lovely woman with a burgeoning career as a commercial writer with a local Vancouver radio station. She very properly left me when I took up with another woman during our marriage. That affair was a disaster even though it lasted over ten years—in the off and on sense. Now I am married to Tammy. She is much younger than I am and a delightful woman with a background in golf management, though she has retired to manage our home lives. She tries to put up with all of my flaws, which must mean she cares about me. Our lives are busy. She loves me. I love her. End of story.

Oh, one more contribution from Denny: he suggested that I could atone for my marital sins by launching a nation-wide "*Mea Culpa*" tour. He would, he promised, supply the t-shirts.

In the area of drink I guess I am my father's son. I have already mentioned his attachment to drink. What I have not said was that in his later years he was unemployed and drank more. Much more. By that time he was living in a boarding house, and in 1972 he died there alone, sitting in a chair with a bottle of whisky beside him.

I was introduced to the hard stuff early in my career while still at CJCS in Stratford, Ontario. At that time it was rye and coke or ginger, graduating to scotch, which anyone can tell you is an acquired taste. I seldom turned down a Drambuie or small glass of grappa, even though the latter had enough potency to burn gaping holes in my esophagus, and I took to drinking brandy at the end of a day to help me, I convinced myself, to sleep better. Who was I kidding? I am, self-admittedly, one of those people who can form habits almost instantly—fortunately, good habits as well as bad. Suffice it to say that, when people close to me started to point out my shortcomings, when I began to realize on my own that I could be putting a very good career in jeopardy, that I was putting friendships at risk, I summoned up the willpower to ease myself in the right direction. But don't get me wrong. I can still indulge in long lunches with the "guys," though it's no longer a huge part of my life.

These days, among my friends, I have a reputation as a hardline wine drinker. I have developed a great fondness for a good quality, robust, cabernet sauvignon from the wine producers in British Columbia or the Napa Valley. As an aside to this, I was recently asked to be one of the judges for the Okanagan Wine Festival. Someone had obviously translated my fondness for wine into an expertise I don't possess, but I felt challenged and ready for a different experience so I said yes. I showed up at the venue for a briefing during which I and the other members of the panel were told what was expected of us. Over the next three days we would be separated into two groups and sequestered in two large suites in the hotel to sniff and spit our way through more than four hundred samples of white and red. For me it was a daunting task. Not so perhaps for my fellow judges, who must have wondered what the hell I was doing among them. They included Tim Pawsey, known for his columns on wine and food in the *Vancouver Courier*; Barbara Philip, the only female master of wine (MW) in the country; Coke Roth, a Washington State lawyer who has an international reputation as a wine judge; Mark Filatow, a Kelowna restauranteur and a member of the International Sommelier Guild; Park Heffelfinger, a man with a sense of humour that matches his size—six-two and wide—and a co-founder of the Vancouver Wine Academy; and others with equally impressive credentials. Marjorie King, who coordinates the event every year, gave me the distinct feeling that I was out of place, given the importance of the judging to the dozens of wine producers in the region. I could hardly blame her.

However, the first day seemed to go well. I was only questioned a couple of times regarding my ratings and I had settled on three all-purpose key words: peach (given to me by my friend Paul Shaw who assured me that it works every time), earthy, and vanilla. Fortunately, I didn't give in to the instinct to swallow and, with the help of a mountain of bread, kept myself from veering out of control and collapsing in a heap on the carpet. But I couldn't help thinking what a shame it was to have this opportunity to indulge and not be able to follow through.

I think my defining moment came on the final day. We were confronted with a flight of (I think) icewines, produced from frozen grapes and commanding very high prices. My first sip filled my mouth with the taste of hops, something I thought surely had no place in this contest. Should I say something to my fellow judges and risk being laughed out of the place, or let it go? Just as I was about to pronounce my findings, Sara D'Amato, a sommelier for

Truffles restaurant in Toronto's Four Seasons Hotel and a well-respected wine writer, beat me to it. She had also found that the wine tasted like beer. I was quietly elated when she confirmed my palate. My place in the wine tasting history of the Okanagan, I thought, was a sure thing. The reality was I had survived an ordeal that was both terrifying and satisfying at the same time.

As for my problem with problem drinking, some of what drove me in that direction I can put down to depression. You wouldn't think, and why should you, that someone who had the measure of success career-wise that I have experienced would suffer from that affliction, but it happened. There I was, seemingly cruising happily along through life, when I crashed. I was a high-profile, highly paid anchor on one of the most successful news programs in North America, and suddenly it didn't seem to mean as much. Nothing made me happy. The things I loved to do, golf and the *News Hour* included, didn't seem to matter anymore. My life became flat, dull and anxiety-ridden. I was enveloped in a blue funk and I couldn't shake it. I'm not known for sharing my problems so I kept this to myself, thinking that no one could have any sympathy for someone who seemed to have it all—or at least most of it. Then I began to think I could drink my way out of it. After that I had good moments but they became fewer as time went on. Relationships began to break apart as I retreated into the shadows. So I drank and let it go on until in desperation

I finally opted for help through my doctor. He asked the expected questions, including the one about thinking of suicide as a means to an end, and I realized I was the text-book case.

There is—for a lot of people who struggle with depression—the feeling that it's a stigma, a mark of weakness and disgrace in the eyes of the rest of society. As a consequence, they suffer in silence. I did, too, until I was given the diagnosis of clinical depression and put on medication. As a result, I regained my equilibrium to the point where I began to shake myself out of the feeling of loss and despair. A lot of self-analysis helped, too, and today, while I still can slip back into the crevasse on occasion, I can almost always pull myself together and get back to life.

To all those who helped me along the way I can only say thanks. And a *mea culpa* to others who suffered because of my depression and my retreat into drinking. They include the women who have shared my life off and on over the years. I treated some badly and was badly treated by others. Nothing can excuse my behaviour at times. I was an out-and-out cad. On the other hand, there were some people who populated my life during those years for a share of the money and the notoriety; to my everlasting grief I let them and so I have only myself to blame.

People usually cringe when I tell them I began smoking when I was nine years old, but the times were different then. The world at large had yet to discover the evils of the habit, and if there were concerns in the medical community at the time that smoking caused cancer or emphysema or asthma or half a dozen other diseases, few people were voicing them. Besides, smoking was deemed "fashionable." My mother smoked as did my father and most of my friends, which is perhaps why I started at such an early age and with no fear of consequence. I began by filching one or two from a packet that my mother left on the kitchen table or the nightstand beside her bed. Of course, we smoked in secrecy, sometimes out of sight by the river in Feversham or under the bridge that crossed the river in town or in some farmer's field or some remote stand of trees where no one ever ventured except our small band of preteen sinners.

We could seldom afford to buy our own. When we could, it was because we pooled our allowances and pretended to the local store owner that we had been sent by our mothers or fathers to bring them home a pack or two. That same store owner was the father of one of my best friends at the time, Steve Eby, so he had access to an unlimited supply of smokes, purloined from the shelves of this father's shop. However, Steve was not really the sharing kind, and he stashed his loot in a barn on the family property or in an all-purpose shed that also housed their toilet facilities— an outhouse that could accommodate, if you can imagine, three people at a time. A three-holer, it was called. (It was very upscale for the times but still a mystery to me. I mean, why would you want to share that kind of intimacy with two other people?) Nevertheless, with a certain amount of detective work, some of us managed to track down Steve's amazing horde of cigarettes and began a phased attack on the goods. Whenever we wanted to smoke, we simply invaded the barn or the shed and took what we needed. We kept the numbers down to ward off suspicion and keep Steve going to the store shelves to replenish his booty. This worked until Steve caught us at it and, in turn, was caught by his father with his hand in the store supply, and it was over for all of us. Steve was put on probation, told to stop smoking and stealing, and we had to find new ways to fuel our habit or go back to actually buying our own.

As time passed, the addiction took hold of me. I smoked for years, even during the *News Hour,* and from time to time some keen-eyed viewer would spot smoke curling up beside me from a cigarette perched in an ashtray, waiting for me to reach down during the next film clip or commercial break. But more than half the people who populated the newsroom at the time were fellow travellers, and on every desk there were ashtrays overflowing with butts and the foul-smelling debris that comes with the habit. By then, though, I was reading more stories on air that warned about the health effects of smoking and about smoking's critical impact on the lives of people who had to breathe the same air as us smokers. The pollution of second-hand smoke had become a real issue, and smokers were quickly becoming the Antichrist. Major campaigns were mounted to prove the error of our indulgence and to convince us to give it up.

I was urged by several friends to surrender and because, I guess, I wanted to set a good example, I began to seek a way out. As any smoker will tell you, it takes a formidable effort. I tried all the pills and potions, the gums and the patches without any luck. Finally, in a fit of desperation I succumbed to a suggestion from my family doctor. He was willing, he said, to help me through the process of butting-out with his newly found skill, hypnosis. At the moment it seemed to be the next thing to voodoo, but it offered the chance of redemption. So during an office visit one day I was put under his spell. It wasn't the show-business, Svengali-type act you might expect but a serious attempt to conquer my mind and defeat the habit. All I can remember was being coaxed into a trance and wondering when I was going to be drifting off into some other world. I think I tried to act like it was working because I didn't want to disappoint the doctor, but it didn't seem like anything was happening. I think I was supposed to sink into unconsciousness because suddenly he told me to wake up. I'm sure I faked that part, but it was what he said next that took hold: "I want you to come back in two weeks' time and be down to two cigarettes a day."

I left his office thinking that this wasn't much of a challenge, that I could lie about it and he would never know the difference. Then something—my conscience, I guess—kicked in and I told myself and Charlie, my cocker spaniel, who had been waiting for me in the car, that the only way to go was cold turkey. The doctor had presented me with a limited supply of Nicoderm, that vile-tasting gum that is designed to wean you off smoking, and I resolved to rely on that and my wavering determination to shun cigarettes once and for all. I ingested tons of the gum over the next month to the point of illness, but it worked. I broke the habit and went smoke-free for years.

Like any other reformed smoker I became a bore to other nicotine slaves, preaching the gospel of non-smoking to anyone who would listen. Not many did or wanted to, but I was satisfied that I had broken my personal barrier and won. At the same time I was honest enough to admit that I could reverse my victory and go back to the noxious habit at any moment, and I often longed for the pleasure of a smoke, especially after a satisfying meal. But I never did give in. At least not to cigarettes. Now, however, I'm smoking again. I discovered—how I'm not quite sure—the delights of a cigar. You think cigarette smoking earned me the total disdain of those around me? Light up a cigar and you instantly become a social pariah. But I understand that—to a degree. Even when I smoked cigarettes, I detested the acrid smell of cigars and was secretly glad that they were banned in certain enclosed areas such as planes or public gathering places. Not anymore. Whereas once I might have led the protest against cigar smoking, waving my placard as I went, I now come firmly down on the side of those who espouse their pleasing taste and satisfaction. I could claim that this turnabout happened as a matter of self-protection against my wife's love of smoking. Tammy smoked when I first met her and has ever since, though she has quit at least a dozen times, using the same nicotine-addiction fighter that I used. However, this would be a pretty weak defence on my part. I actually didn't need a whole lot of encouragement to smoke cigars.

Today I obey the rules, staying the required six metres from air intakes in public buildings, lighting up al fresco and as far away from others as I can get and being entirely considerate of the comfort of others. Of course, sometimes it's not enough. I have a healthy habit of walking most mornings, sometimes even in the rain, along the seawall near my home. As I trudge to and from the park, I puff happily on a Cohiba or Don Tomas Macanudo. I call this a "healthy habit" but truly I walk and smoke to save my neighbours from the stench of my indulgence as the smoke would waft into their open apartment windows from my courtyard below. Still, a little exercise doesn't hurt. But while I think I'm doing the right thing, other people, mostly the spandex-clad runners who populate the seawall, definitely aren't sure. More than once I've heard the whispered word "disgusting" darted in my direction or have seen the twisted faces of displeasure as they pass, trying to avoid the emissions. Once from a more practical opponent came the words "waste of money" as she deliberately crossed the sidewalk in front of me.

However, there have been occasions when others have professed their love of the smell, and some have stopped to compare notes on the delights of the habit. Not often, mind you, but enough times to buoy my spirits and reinforce my pleasure. And sometimes when I stop to rest on an empty, secluded park bench and I'm lost in the moment, I look down at the scattering of cigarette butts around my feet to see if there is the stub of an old cigar among them. I can't claim to have seen one yet, and I could argue that this proves one of the merits of cigars in that they are entirely composed of tobacco held together by another layer of tobacco and therefore, if they ever do end up in a flower bed or garden or on the green lawns of some par, they will decompose to fulfill another function as fertilizer. Perhaps that's why they are tolerated on the golf courses of the nation, which actually, while not approving of cigars, cater to the habit by selling them in their pro shops.

On the health side one does not—or certainly should not—inhale cigar smoke so that the wear and tear on the internal organs, especially the lungs, is mitigated. Yes, I know there are other forms of cancer that can come into play where the tongue and other mouth parts are involved, but you seldom hear of those afflictions. And, by the way, did you ever see a magazine entirely devoted to cigarette smoking? I doubt it. But cigar smokers have a number of publications that deal solely with their habit: *Cigar Aficionado*, for instance, rates cigars as *Wine Spectator* rates wines. When Barack Obama gained the White House, the magazine leapt into the political arena, stating its case for the return to normal relations with Cuba for the benefit of cigar lovers in the United States who have been denied their coveted Cuban cigars since the Kennedy administration slapped an embargo on Cuba after the failure of the Bay of Pigs invasion. No word from the current White House yet. But American cigar lovers live in hope.

Lest you think I'm just another smoky voice in the wilderness when it comes to these issues, let me quote from an article titled "Walking my Cigar," published in a 1992 issue of the same magazine and written by a much better-known and more skilled writer than myself, Gay Talese, himself a devout cigar smoker. He talks about an encounter on fabled, toney Park Avenue in New York City, where he walked his two Australian terriers every evening in order to enjoy his daily smoke. One night as he walked past the dining patio of a local restaurant, he became aware of "two female diners, not only holding their noses but waving their hands over their plates of food and wine glasses as a way of nullifying what they presumably feared to be the floating poison of my cigar smoke." And he goes on:

> Just as I passed their table one of the women exclaimed, "Ugh!"
>
> "Are you referring to my cigar, Madam?" I asked, pausing to remove my $7 Macanudo Vintage Number One while pulling back on the leash of my growling Australian terriers.
>
> "Yes," she said. "I find it offensive. In fact, it stinks."
>
> "This is a public street, you know," I said.
>
> "Yes," she said, "and I'm part of the public."
>
> I was tempted to inhale and blow smoke in her direction, which hardly would have downgraded the air quality of the avenue, where the soot from the uptown buses and cars had already turned the café's white tablecloths toward shades of battleship gray and navy blue. But I noticed the woman's companion, who had not ceased wringing her hands over her dinner, had now drawn the attention of the waiter and some other people at the next table, and suspecting I would have few allies in this crowd, I allowed my dogs to pull me farther downtown.

In the text that follows, Talese tries to explain the growth of the rampant anti-cigar attitude in America, suggesting it could lie in the spread of female sexism that has women getting back at their "cigar-chomping, tough-minded, sexist fathers who, refusing to pass on that lucrative family business to a worthy daughter, favoured instead an incompetent son." And Talese wonders, "What would Sigmund Freud, an inveterate cigar smoker, say to all this? Would he identify the cigar as a phallic symbol that contemporary women both envy and loathe?" Talese admits that criticism of his habit doesn't necessarily come from women alone, and that he's been confronted by other men. But he ends by arguing that:

> The cigar is becoming increasingly a less portable pleasure, and in my view this is but one symptom of a growing neo-Puritanism and negativism that has choked the nation with codes of correctness, and has led to greater mistrust between the sexes, and has finally, in the name of health and virtue and fairness, reduced options and pleasures that, in measured amounts, had once been generally accepted as normal and natural.

For my part, I can see that in the days to come cigar smokers like myself and Talese will become the ultimate social enemy. Perhaps we'll be transported in a dun-coloured shuttle bus to a designated field in the Fraser Valley, there to spend sixty minutes or so indulging our habit in a billowing cloud of offensive smoke, grousing to each other about our fate but satisfied in a grudging way that we are keeping our enemies, the non-cigar smokers, out of harm's way. Or it could be a floating barge service to the centre of English Bay or our own mountaintop retreat, set aside by a benign government, where we could smoke our brains out while some faceless DJ plays "On Top of Old Smokey." We will be endlessly isolated but at least not subjecting our critics or anyone else to the evils of that which gives us such pleasure.

Excuse me now while I get down from my soapbox.

11

And on a Lighter Note

I SUPPOSE THAT EVERYONE at sometime in their lives thinks they can play a musical instrument. My mother certainly thought my sisters were capable when she arranged accordion lessons for Anne and Phyllis. Fortunately for all of us their attention span waned quickly and we were spared the cacophony. Some twenty-odd years ago it occurred to me, for no obvious reason, that I could become a guitar player, though not just a guitar, but an acoustic guitar and I would specialize in classical music. To that end I sought out a teacher and settled on Walter, whose last name escapes me, and took my first lesson in the living room of his house in the Dunbar area of Vancouver. I was a poor student and I found my teacher to be less than enthusiastic and perhaps a little dour in his approach. After a few lessons I left to find someone else to torture.

I was given the name of a young fellow who had a

reputation as a thoroughly talented musician. He had "busker" experience around the world and he agreed to take me on with my first lesson scheduled for October 1, 1983 in his Richmond home. Michael Friedman and I hit it off immediately. We began with scales and simple chords and over the course of almost four years, to July 17, 1987, I progressed to actual pieces by Handel and Bach and even Beethoven. I was not Carnegie Hall-ready but I had, I thought, achieved a level that was both satisfying and enjoyable. I was so engrossed in playing that I took the guitar almost everywhere I went. I recall lugging it to Toronto for some kind of network meeting and ordering up a cab to the airport at the end of my stay. For some reason my transportation turned out to be a white Rolls Royce and I sat in the back with my guitar propped up beside me. As we drove out of the city, I sensed that cars were pulling up beside us and peering into the back of my limo to see if some kind of celebrity was on his way to the airport. I waved, they saw the guitar, and for a fleeting moment I was a "rock star." After that, my ardour slowly cooled. I still have my guitar—in fact, three or four of them—and even though I haven't picked any of them up in ages, I always think that if I ever retire altogether, I'll track Michael Friedman down and stoke that smouldering talent once again.

I'm known among my friends and family as a bit of a collector. I have a collection of lead soldiers, those miniature military figures that were the feature of many a childhood in England and elsewhere. I also have a few teddy bears strewn around my home, and I have a minor collection of art, mostly Canadian with the emphasis on British Columbia.

The lead soldiers marched into my life in the sixties when I was assigned to do a story on the sudden rise in value of what people generally call "toy soldiers." To beef up my story I did a search of some Toronto antique shops and managed to come up with a few figures that had somehow found their way from someone's attic or old toy box. My research also determined that most makers of soldiers were steering away from lead and had started to use plastic in their moulds. I was told it was being done in the interest of safety, that too many children had taken to gnawing on their little troops, risking their lives by ingesting the lead. The rumour was that one of the British royals had raised the alarm when a prince or princess, I never found out which, had become ill after chewing on a lancer mounted on a brown horse. I speculated on that last bit, but it occurred to me that it would be fun, if not profitable, to start my own collection. I had never had any of these things in my years as a kid in the UK so it would be a chance to fill that gap in my evolution.

A firm known as William Britain Limited was the prime producer of the figurines and had led the market in the production of non-leaded pieces and hollow-casting, which was a way of reducing the lead content, before it turned its production completely over to plastic. But it was only the production before that move that counted as collectible. I began with a couple of "less than mint" pieces, Grenadier

Guards with peeling paint and, in one case, a missing arm. Then as I became more absorbed in the hobby, I started to ferret out the good stuff. I learned that what you go for are sets of "Britains" still in their original packaging and untouched by playful hands. Over the years I managed to enhance my collection with a few prime pieces.

Hal Jackman, a Toronto financier, and Malcolm Forbes, the ultra-rich American who created *Forbes* magazine, had massive collections. Forbes kept his soldiers in a specially built castle in Morocco. I kept mine in a large wooden box and later in a spiffy display case. Prized among my pieces are eight military skiers clad in white coveralls and hoods and a complete replica of the royal carriage used for the Queen's coronation in 1953 with the horses that pulled it down the Mall and around Trafalgar Square. It came to me in a quite unusual way. I got a call in the newsroom one day from a man who had read somewhere about my soldiers and said that he had something I might be interested in. Not wanting to offend him, I said he should come by the TV station in Burnaby and I'd have a look. He showed up a day or two later, cradling the royal carriage and all its bits and bobs in a shallow, crumbling cardboard box. I paid him three hundred dollars on the spot. My mother, with her royalist leanings, would have been pleased with that acquisition.

I mentioned my collection of teddy bears, but they were more an accident or, if you like, an unintended accumulation. In the late seventies someone gave me a stuffed bear, an expensive one, as a birthday present. It was a toy that had been created to mark the impending hundredth anniversary of one of the great bear makers in the world, the Steiff Company of Germany. Since it was the Rolls Royce of bears, it had a small place of honour in my apartment. But just the sight of it apparently gave everyone else the idea that I collected bears, and soon the population increased tenfold. I finally had to put a stop to it by faking my absolute lack of interest in bears of any shape and size and donating my little stuffed friends to a children's charity.

My sporting life, if that's what you can call it, actually began when I moved to the West Coast. I took up tennis and joined a club dedicated to the game. Then I decided to try my hand at skiing. I drove up to Whistler one weekend with friends, rented some gear, bought a day pass, tried not to break my neck and left that same day completely besotted with the experience. Within three weeks I had signed up for lessons, bought all the necessary equipment and, believe it or not, a ski condo. Roy Ferris, a fixture at Whistler almost from its beginnings, offered to coach me, and soon I could make it down most of the intermediate terrain without having to pick myself up every hundred yards. Roy, a Brit like myself, had begun his skiing on Ben Nevis in Scotland, skied most of the elite European resorts when he wasn't helping out in the family pub in London, then came to Canada where, among other things, he established a summer ski school on Whistler Mountain, employing as part of his instruction team Toni Sailer, the Olympic skier from Austria. Roy was a great teacher and dazzling to watch whenever he navigated the most challenging runs. But I was a fair-weather skier. If the sun wasn't shining on the slopes and the snow wasn't the texture of soft butter, I stayed in the valley in front of the fire at my newly acquired condo or at the nearest, most comfortable bar. I had no problem handling après-ski. But eventually I gave up skiing and spent my summers rather than my winters in Whistler, upgraded to bigger and better—and more expensive—condos then, when the real estate market went through the roof, I cashed in and left.

However, summers at Whistler were idyllic. You could even ski on the glaciers to a point, but by then golf was my game, if not my passion. Although it's long been a fantasy of mine to become a reasonably good golfer, I fear it will never happen. I didn't really get involved in the game until late in life. I had dabbled at it back in Ontario but never had time to devote the hours and the attention it requires. It wasn't until I signed on with BCTV to do the *News Hour* that I organized my work day to include some time on the driving range or the course. What really set the wheels in motion was a playing lesson, more or less, with Jim McLaughlin, who was then the pro at the University Golf Course. His family, beginning with his dad Jack, had a long and auspicious history with the game. Paul Shaw, my friend of many years and the negotiator of all my contracts with BCTV and later Global BC, was with us on that occasion, and it was at his urging that Jim started to offer me some pointers. I can't remember which hole we were on, but as the direct result of Jim's pointers, I managed to land a shot on the green from a fair distance down the fairway and from then on I was hooked. (That's probably not a term one should use when talking about golf so I will correct that to say my pursuit of the game became a lot more intense.)

I now play a lot in charity tournaments for any number of causes and I enjoy them immensely. Over the years I must have played with scores of different people, and I can truly say that I've never met a golfer I didn't like, such is the camaraderie of the game. Even though they may come to the course expecting me to outplay them, I usually disappoint them. I can't live up to my unearned reputation of being good at the game. But if nothing else, I am well connected to golf. My wife Tammy spent twenty years in the business, rising from a member of the grounds crew at Gallagher's Canyon in Kelowna to her long-time role as manager of that course and a thirty-six-hole layout now known as the Okanagan Golf Club. She comes from a golfing family: her father, Dick Munn, is an icon in the sport. At one time the pro at the prestigious Point Grey Golf Club in Vancouver and at other equally established courses before that, he (with a group of like-minded friends and business partners) founded Gallagher's and is to this day, though retired, a sought-after teacher and designer in the field. He is selective about taking on students but in recent times has coached me and sorted out some of the obvious defects in my swing. I still haven't quite managed to advance beyond the mediocre stage, though by my own standards I have more moments of brilliance than I used to have. In fact, after a round with

Dick and a couple of his pals in Arizona, my coach said, as we wrapped up eighteen, "You hit a lot of good shots today." High praise, indeed. But just to show you how frail my game is, I played a number of charity golf tournaments after that and retreated to all of my faults. On the first few holes I seemed to know what I was doing, then "the wheels came off." If you're my calibre of golfer, God forbid, you may understand my frustration. But it never takes away from my enjoyment of the game or the belief that, if I spend endless hours on the practice tee, I will yet rise above my shortcomings. I'd better hurry up.

As for the charity aspect of golf, I'm thankful to have been involved in the raising of hundreds of thousands of dollars. I have my name on a fundraising tournament with my old friend Neal Macrae, the acerbic sports broadcaster for CKNW in Vancouver, a man with a heart of gold, who is (I think) a master of shtick when it comes to his audience. With the help and expertise of another friend, Barry McPherson, we've staged sixteen tournaments, including one to help the victims of the devastating fires that swept the North Okanagan in 2003. On one tournament day we raised, with the help of some generous corporations, more than six hundred thousand dollars. Was it Twain who described the game as "a good walk spoiled"? So much for that.

Other than my truncated career in the peewee hockey league when I was ten or eleven, I have never aspired to be a hero on ice, though I did try briefly again after my celebrity came into play, popping up in a few areas of the province, such as 100 Mile House, to play charity games, fundraisers for local groups. Our BCTV team, dubbed the "Tubes," were a fairly rag-tag bunch, but we had a core of competent players. I was not one of them. In fact, I will always be remembered, to my everlasting shame, as the Tube who scored on his own goal. I was assigned the job of defenceman, and I remember being caught in a sudden onrush of opposition players on a breakaway. I was the Tubes' last, lonely line of defence—only me between the opposition and a possible goal—and somehow when the lead skater let a rocket go off the end of his stick, I got a piece of the puck. The force almost sent me sprawling on the ice, but I managed to lash out at the puck, hoping it would veer toward the boards, thus making me a hero or, at the very least, the star player of the game. Fate made it otherwise. The puck shot off my stick, hit the goalpost and ricocheted into the net, right past our exasperated goalie, Mike Johnston, generally known as "Tiny." He was a huge hulk of man who filled the crease with about 240 pounds of flesh plus huge pads that were wrapped around legs bigger than tree stumps. It wasn't a winning goal for the other side, but it was enough to send them to a decisive victory by a margin of a dozen goals. If it hadn't been for the comedic aspect of it, I might have skipped the post-game party, but Mike never let me forget the incident. Until the recent day when he died from pancreatic cancer, he never missed a chance to remind me of my lack of talent and that dreadful night. From then on I became a committed spectator.

But while I may not play the game and I may have divided loyalties—given the enthusiasm I shared with my mother for the Leafs and for my home team, the Vancouver Canucks—I still have an interest in the game. Recently two of my dearest friends, the Moscone brothers, Sandy and Mike, Leafs fans forever, gave me a share of the ownership of the Grandview Steelers, a junior B team of some distinction. In his younger years Mike played for the Steelers as did his two sons, and both Mike and Sandy have coached the game. In fact, in 2002 Mike Moscone was named "Coach of the Year" by the BC Amateur Hockey Association for his efforts to improve the skills of his young team members and to prepare some—for example, Milan Lucic, who now steers the puck around the ice for the Boston Bruins—for the National Hockey League careers for which they and their parents yearn.

The Steelers association was formed in 1967 and played in the Trout Lake Arena attached to the Grandview Community Club until the 2003–04 season when they moved to the Britannia Community Centre. Then in 2007–08 under the Moscones' aegis they were moved from East Vancouver to nicer digs at the Burnaby Winter Club, and the facilities there were brought up to a new standard. The huge locker room was updated and now it even has flat-screen TVs that in the pre-game anticipation period often carry inspirational, sports-related movies to get the players psyched up before the puck is dropped. I dropped in one Sunday afternoon and caught them watching the 1940 Warner Brothers film *Knute Rockne, All American*, which starred Pat O'Brien in the title role and Ronald Reagan as his star linebacker, George Gipp, more affectionately known as "The Gipper." I have to say that perhaps on that occasion at least, the movie message was lost as the Steelers lost that Sunday afternoon game, and the year ended with them on the outside looking in while the rest of the league moved on to the playoffs. However, in the previous season, the first year of my co-ownership with the Moscone brothers, they were a team to be reckoned with. They won the regional and provincial championships that year and came third in the national championship tournament in Brandon, Manitoba. It was a heady year for everyone, players, coaches and owners alike. Now all of us sport those oversized, Stanley Cup-like rings, bigger than a boulder, that are emblematic of a win at the provincial level. I seldom wear mine since I can barely lift my arm when it's on my finger, but I'm very proud of it and our Steelers.

Among my friends and acquaintances are a number of men who are connected to the big league game. I've always been a fan of Trevor Linden and Darcy Rota and especially of old-timers Stan Smyl and Dennis Kearns. If I had a dream Canucks team, Tiger Williams would be on it, and it would be coached by Pat Quinn with Marc Crawford as assistant coach. I'd make Brian Burke general manager because I like him and he had the good fortune to marry Jennifer Mather, an extremely talented broadcaster I was smart enough to have hired years ago to be a weather person on our channel. Of course, by then I'd have taken over ownership from Francesco Aquilini and his family and we would be on better terms. For years Francesco has harboured an extreme dislike of the media—though not me in particular. But back in the '80s when we did a series of reports on his father, Luigi, and his then-business partner, Giovanni Zen, and their dealings with their tenants in a group of rundown apartment buildings, I'm sure it had an impact on the then much younger Francesco. The reports were factual and were of necessity "lawyered" before they went to air, so we felt right in making some fairly strong criticisms of the two partners. Afterward, we might have been threatened with legal action, but to my recollection the challenge went nowhere.

Perhaps it was our description of Zen and Aquilini that stung Francesco, but ever since then he has tried to steer clear of nosey journalists, especially those of the electronic type, and now with the ownership of the Canucks in his grasp, he is highly critical of sportswriters and reporters as well. It seems to have never dawned on Francesco that, if you want to a live a quiet, reclusive life, you damn sure want to stay out of the glare of the public spotlight. And the very last thing you want to do if you have a need for that kind of privacy is own a hockey team, especially one with fans as rabid as Canucks fans are. In any case, I'm convinced that—with a few exceptions—ownership of a high-profile sports team is a matter of ego, but a lot more goes with the franchise than goodwill and happiness. It makes me want to take Francesco out to lunch one day and tell him, as soothingly as possible, that the media is not out to get him or his family for any reason, real or imagined. It's just what we do.

12

Every Dog Has Its Day

I CAN'T REMEMBER MANY DAYS in my life that didn't include the happy presence of a dog. In my childhood days in England it was a cocker spaniel called Daisy. There were other dogs after Daisy and even another Daisy, also a cocker spaniel, who was brought into our home by my father who had a sort of grudging affection for dogs but never let them forget who filled the bowl or paid the veterinarian bills. His anger with them, for whatever reason, sometimes reached that level usually reserved for the human transgressors in his life, and many a dog got to know the toe of my father's boot.

But it is the last two dogs with whom I've shared my life that have been undeniably special. Charlie, yet another cocker spaniel, came to have more fans than many of us in this business can claim. Our relationship began in 1996 after I mentioned to Eileen Dreever, who regularly appeared on our *Noon News* program in an attempt to find adoptive owners for abandoned and unwanted dogs, cats, and even Vietnamese pigs—which were popular for a while during the eighties—that if she ever came across a cocker spaniel looking for a home, I might be interested. Sure enough, shortly afterward, she appeared at my office door with the most soulful, lost-looking creature I'd ever seen. It took just seconds for me to make up my mind about Charlie, and the years we spent together were, I think, a love story.

Not long after Charlie arrived, the station was targeted for a strike by technical employees, editorial staff, reporters and on-air talent. As a newly minted member of the management team, I was exempt, but it did complicate my life because the first strike day coincided almost exactly with my adoption of Charlie and the picketing meant a longer work day. I was living alone at the time, and doggy daycare as we now know it wasn't available then. I certainly couldn't leave the dog alone in my apartment for seven or eight hours or in my car in the parking lot at the TV station, and I couldn't inflict him on a friend or neighbour when I wasn't sure that he didn't have some dark character flaw I hadn't yet detected. So off he went to be by my side in the office until the day the labour strife was all ironed out. Charlie couldn't have been happier. During the strike, which lasted as I recall less than a week, Charlie identified his role in the newsroom, and the moment that routine was established, he fashioned himself a new lifestyle, becoming a star in his own right. When I left my office and headed for the news set, Charlie was right there with me, trotting through the newsroom, jumping onto the set and settling down at my feet. He slept through my every word until he heard me say goodnight. Then he would get up, shake himself awake and lead me back across the newsroom to my office, waiting there until he heard the jangle of my car keys, which he knew meant we were on our way home. That routine would be a major part of his life for the next six or seven years.

To this day I believe that his being there humanized the workplace and made it a more comfortable place to be. However, his presence went undetected by our viewers until somehow his story got out and his fan base expanded. After that we would occasionally take a shot of him in the final moments of the *News Hour,* and the legend grew to a point where, if he wasn't shown from time to time or at least mentioned, there would be inquiries as to his whereabouts and his well-being. He even became the subject of a Mike McCardell story. Mike, as many of our viewers know, does a nightly story just before we close off. They are a joy for people who watch the program as most of them are serendipitous and deal with ordinary people and their lives. They are, as well, the product of the most inquiring mind in the business. Back in 1976 when the *Vancouver Sun* was strikebound, Mike, a transplanted New Yorker and a reporter for that paper, grew restless with the protest situation there and asked for a temporary position with us. It turned into a lasting, very successful association.

Mike's story on Charlie touched on one strange but significant trait in the dog: he was calm by nature, but when he heard a doorbell, he became the ultimate canine enforcer, determined to protect his territory and his family. As a result, at the outset we were all fearful that he might suddenly have a fit of barking during the show and betray his presence, but as the years went by, it never happened and we relaxed. Mike used this as the centrepiece of his report, conspiring with our audio operator to play the sound of a doorbell during a commercial break in the *News Hour*. Charlie fell for it and went berserk. When it was played back in Mike's report, the audience loved it and Charlie even more.

As in most adoption cases, dogs and otherwise, the origin of the adoptee is seldom revealed. That was the case with Charlie. I always wondered about it but couldn't get an answer from the SPCA. Perhaps they really didn't know, but if they did, they weren't about to tell me. But I found out, I think, along the way. I have no way to authenticate the claim that came in a letter sent to my office one day, but it came from a fellow who wrote at length and enclosed photos to tell me that he was Charlie's previous human. (That's the way we dog owners talk.) He had been, he said, a sidewalk artist trying to make a living in Gastown, and Charlie had been his sidekick, luring people and perhaps a few coins with his typical Charlie cuteness. But, the writer explained, his wife had become pregnant, and after the child was born, they could see no way, financially or otherwise, that they could care for both animal and baby, and they decided to give up Charlie for adoption. Knowing Charlie as I did, I can only imagine what a heart-wrenching decision that must have been. (I've since joked that, had I been them, I might have opted for the reverse.) In any case, I have no reason to doubt the letter writer's story.

The pictures sure looked like Charlie, and everyone, even a dog, has to start somewhere. Charlie went on to become a cover dog for magazines, the subject of other television shows, and, I suspect, the envy of every other dog in British Columbia. His death, from the complications of old age, left a definite void in my life. But not for long.

Enter Jack. You might say that Jack is my "step-dog" inasmuch as I inherited his affection when Tammy and I were married a few years ago. She had adopted him when he was a pup and loved and trained him well. You must forgive the bragging, but he is an exceptional animal, smart beyond belief and sensitive to a fault. Officially described on his veterinary papers as a Maltese cross, he is the kind of dog that you can take anywhere—and we often do. It helps that he is tiny and well-behaved and now very popular with our viewers. He came to be that way by simply and amazingly taking over where Charlie, so to speak, left off. From the first day I took him to the office he seemed to sense that he had a purpose in being there and that was to assume the role that Charlie had created. He performed it without missing a beat. He followed me as I walked to my desk on the set that day, plunked himself down at my feet and promptly fell asleep. He came back to life when he heard me say goodnight, and he's been doing that, Charlie-style, ever since.

Sometimes I think his fan base is much broader than my own. Recently the British Columbia Institute of Technology (BCIT) saw fit to award me an honorary doctorate. I was flattered to say the least. On the day of the ceremony Tammy and I and, of course, Jack, went to the school for the convocation exercise, but we intended, as we sometimes do, to leave the dog in the car, making sure (in case the SPCA is wondering) that he was cool and comfortable. But when certain faculty members found out he was with us, nothing would do but we should bring him into the school and let him share in the honours. They insisted it wouldn't be right if Jack, as long as he was there, wasn't part of the day. Jack seemed to think so, too. Post-ceremony, he took over the spotlight to the point that the photographs taken that day of myself signing the register include, front and centre, the family dog. He does a "star turn" as well on the annual Variety Club Telethon known as the Show of Hearts, to critical acclaim. We regularly get pleading phone calls from viewers who want to see him every night on the *News Hour*, which would be a bit much I think, but there's no doubt he's a popular part of local television lore. Maybe it's his underbite that endears him to so many, including Deb Hope, who as the saying goes "loves him to death."

13

Making Movies

MOVIES HAVE BEEN A PART OF MY LIFE since I was a boy in England. Sixpence and a new feature at the local Odeon were my mother's way of getting me out of the house and her hair on a Saturday afternoon. Even today I'm the first one to my local electronics shop on Tuesdays when newly released DVDs go on sale. And movies became, in a minor way, an adjunct to my production career because it's not unusual in our business for the local news anchor to be cast in a film production as, you guessed it, a news anchor. My first casting call came in Toronto in 1973. The film was called *To Kill the King*, and it was shooting in our CFTO studios in Agincourt, just outside of Toronto, that location being chosen because this was to be the first full-length feature film shot entirely on videotape. It was a big deal then though not so much these days when many so-called Movies of the Week are done that way. The star of the film was the British-born actor Barry Morse, who had made his name on television in the highly successful 1963–67 ABC series *The Fugitive* as Lieutenant Gerard, the policeman who constantly pursued Dr. Richard Kimble, played by David Janssen. In *To Kill the King* he portrayed an American presidential secretary involved in a mix of foreign and political intrigue, and I was the television reporter and anchor who followed his story. I never actually saw Mr. Morse, never shared the sound stage with him and never saw the completed film. Just as well, I suppose, since it sank without distinction. The only thing I found intriguing about the whole affair was the process of dubbing, which is when an actor is asked to sit in a recording studio and provide dialogue while watching his character's lips move on screen. For some reason I enjoyed the process and got high praise from director George McCowan, who said I had achieved in only a couple of takes what some actors take hours to perfect. He didn't comment on my acting.

I was called on a few more times for films and even worked with actor/director Sean Penn on a film called *The Pledge*, filmed mostly on BC's Sunshine Coast in 2000. It starred such luminaries as Jack Nicholson, Helen Mirren, Vanessa Redgrave and Mickey Rourke, none of whom I ever saw during the filming. But Penn was there in our BCTV studios when I did my bit—yes, once again as a news anchor. It was shot on our regular set with a teleprompter, and the whole thing was over in a matter of minutes. Penn was effusive in his praise for my performance, but then how difficult can it be a for a news anchor to act as a news anchor? I've been doing that for longer than he's been in pictures.

I was thankful for his high rating, though, and the cheque, which was somewhere around $2,400. Occasionally I still get a small residual fee for my efforts, the last one coming to about $24, but in American funds.

A year after *The Pledge* came *Saving Silverman*, one of those often popular teenage comedy productions. I was typecast again and this time pocketed a tidy $1,100 for about an hour's work. However, my only satisfactory role as a news anchor in movies was in a cartoon series on the Family Channel. It was called *Being Ian* and I played myself, Tony Parsons, as a caricature. It was actually fun.

My body of movie work, such as it was, was further enhanced—and you know I'm joking—by an appearance on *The 4400*, the very popular sci-fi series that ran from 2004 to 2007 on the USA Network. It chronicled the reappearance of 4,400 people who had disappeared from the earth over the years and then returned in a blinding flash, unchanged in age and appearance. This was my break-out role—I played, not a news anchor, but a talk-show host trying to unravel the mystery of these strange non-aliens. I forget what they paid me, but the experience was excruciating. The old saying "hurry up and wait" was never so true as on the *4400* set. I had my own trailer/dressing room but it was a barren affair furnished with a decrepit television set, a fridge loaded with bottled water and a toilet that had seen better days—or at least one would hope. My call time was ten in the morning. My first appearance on the set was about four in the afternoon, by which time I was totally bored, tired and in such a bad frame of mind that I completely forgot my dialogue, even though I'd spent most of the waiting hours rehearsing myself for my "moment." Eventually I did what I had to but without much feeling or believability, and afterward I was cranky and anxious to go home and forget the whole experience. Another small cheque followed but no directorial acclaim. And that was my last go-round with the movies. As an aside to that adventure, however, I didn't realize until much later that one of the actors with an ongoing role in the four seasons of the series was a young woman named Samantha Ferris whose father, Roy Ferris, taught me to ski all those years ago at Whistler. For a while she had also been a weather person on our *Noon News* program.

There was one more event in my life that involved a movie, but I was on the producing side that time along with Pamela Martin. This one was the brainchild of cameraman Len Kowalewich, and the one thing that it taught me was that my place was in front of the camera doing the news, not venturing into such unknown territory. The year was 1975 and I had just switched from CTV West Coast bureau chief to BCTV anchorman. Cameron Bell, my new boss, tried to warn me away from it by telling me that if it failed, as it surely would, it would be a definite blot on my copy book. But I insisted and went ahead.

The project was a dream Len had been nurturing for years. It was to be called *The Columbia Connection*, and you can guess by the title that it was another film about evil and intrigue among drug dealers and the renowned cartel from South America. For star power we hired Britt Ekland, who must have been desperate for work at the time. It might have been the highlight of the whole dubious adventure when Len invited me to Los Angeles to be on hand when she signed her contract, probably because I had put up fourteen thousand dollars of her upfront fee of twenty-five thousand dollars, which, as far as I know, was all she ever received. The deal was signed in one of those swanky Beverly Hills restaurants and again in Vancouver at an equally swanky eatery that existed under the Umberto's banner. I expect the double-signing was as much for show as anything and to attract more investors. Did it work? I doubt it.

Her co-star was a then-little-known Canadian actor named Winston Rekert who later earned well-deserved recognition in a long series of US and Canadian television dramas and films, including the 1987 film *Adderly*, for which he won a Gemini, and the 1990–95 Canadian television series *Neon Rider*. Suffice it to say, he now has a long credit list and excellent acting credentials. We filled out the cast with Leon Bibb who, during his career in the States had been the opening act for singer Harry Belafonte; by the time we came into his life with *The Columbia Connection* he was a fixture in Vancouver theatre, having been one of the stars of the Vancouver Arts Club's 1972 production of *Jacques Brel is Alive and Well and Living in Paris*. Jackson Davies, who would go on to star in *The Beachcombers*, also joined us as did Annie Kidder, Margot's younger sister.

The film was shot in Mexico, and that's where the first signs of trouble began. The Mexican authorities were on side when it came to having us there, even though they knew their country was just a stand-in for South America, but we had to pay the price by greasing the palms of the lesser officials who held out their hands at every opportunity. This whole "grease" proposition went all the way down the food chain, and no one could refuse. It was the way things got done there, virtually without exception, but this problem ate such a very large hole in our budget that, in desperation and in an attempt to keep the project afloat, I handed over thousands of dollars to Len to apply to it. He kicked in some of his own money and probably mortgaged his home to pay the bills, and somehow got the film made. I never saw any accounting and really didn't want to know about it because in the end I sued him for the fourteen thousand dollars I had put up to pay Britt Ekland's signing fee. When I won the case, he agreed to pay me so much a month until the debt was satisfied. I never felt good about the suit, but I knew I'd never see a penny from the film and I didn't feel like making a donation of that size, even though I knew Len was left without much of a bank balance in the end.

The film never saw the light of day as *The Columbia Connection*. Instead it was released in 1975 as *Dead Wrong* and even played in the UK where they changed the title to *Entrapment*, perhaps to protect the innocent. Apparently it is still available for home consumption as *Death Be Not Proud*. A couple of footnotes to this sad affair: The part of the news anchor in the film was played by Wayne Cox; I hope he got paid. And Britt Ekland's character was named Priscilla "Penny" Lancaster, which, in case you didn't know, is the name of Rod Stewart's current wife. Was Britt taking a poke at her ex at our expense, I wonder? In any case, I have never run across anyone who has actually seen the movie nor do I want to, and until now just one person outside of the cast and crew ever knew I had been involved.

14

A Short Chapter on a Long-Standing Gripe

I AM BY NO STRETCH OF THE IMAGINATION an arbiter of the English language or an authority on correct grammatical usage and/or pronunciation. But it seems to me that the least we can do, those of us who put a certain amount of pride in our daily contribution to electronic journalism, is brush up on the very basics of these important facets of our jobs.

For example, I hate finding redundancies in my script such as the NDP party or an ATM machine. Errors such as these slip into story introductions more often than you might imagine. And it happens in print as well. I think I've lost the argument at BCTV over the correct use of the words "further" and "farther," but I scored a victory when it came to the word "fortuitous," which means "accidental" and not "fortunate." There also seems to be some confusion over the correct usage of the expressions "at present" and "presently." I've often heard on-air presenters announce that the temperature is "presently" eighteen—or ten or fourteen—degrees. Wrong! "Presently" refers to the future and means "soon." For example, "The Queen will be here presently." When one speaks of the current temperature, it should be—if the term is used at all—"at present." And nobody can convince me that "horrific" has a place in the English language when it comes to describing the carnage of a traffic accident. Perhaps "horrible" or "horrifying" is suitable for the occasion but not a word that sounds as if it was fabricated by someone whose breath was taken away by the sheer tragedy of the event and simply reached out for a new superlative, plucked it from the air and slammed it into a sentence. But I hear this word time and time again on local stations and on the big nets, so I guess that everyone but me has accepted it.

I am also pretty much alone, it seems, when it comes to the pronunciation of "kilometres." For me it has always been "kil'-o-metres," with the accent on the first syllable, which makes much more sense than what I normally hear, which is, to use a bit of phonetics, "kil-om'-etres" with the emphasis on the second syllable. The best argument against the latter pronunciation is that, if the accent should be on the second syllable, why don't we say "kil-oss'-cyles" rather than "kil'-o-cycles" or "kil-og'-grams" instead of "kil'-o-grams"? Of course, the argument for the pronunciation that I rail against goes something like "Well, everyone else says it that way, so who am I to change it?" But I say that wrong is wrong, though I do keep in mind that common usage often forges its own rules. Sometimes, in fact, it becomes a matter of two pronunciations being acceptable. You will remember, I'm sure, the old Gershwin brothers' song "Let's Call the Whole Thing Off," and the lyrics, "You like potato and I like potahto, you like tomato and I like tomahto." The verses do make a point, I guess, but some of us continue to fight the good fight.

Sometimes, in broadcasting, it is the words that are omitted that cause problems, especially when it comes to news anchors like me who prefer not to read the script until actually taking it to air, thinking, as I do, that we like to hear it for the first time just as the viewer at home is hearing it. For me it enhances the storytelling aspect of being a competent anchor as the viewers and I go through an hour of sharing information and facts. Of course, that approach can sometimes cause problems as it did recently during a week-long series on an annual awards program that honours people in the community who have over-come adversity of one form or another to bravely rise above their problems and achieve significant milestones in their lives. This program, called "The Courage to Come Back," is one of Deb Hope's pet projects, and she takes a keen interest in the whole process of gathering the names of the nominees, interviewing each one, then telling their stories one at a time over the five nights prior to the actual awards ceremony, which she emcees. On a recent show I introduced one of her stories and fell afoul of a writer's slip-up and my own penchant for not pre-reading the script. I cruised through the introduction unaware that the writer had left out the word "back" in the title of the event. I could hear the laughter and the twittering behind me from the newsroom when I announced that the annual awards for "The Courage to Come" were being handed out the following week. I didn't check to see how many phone calls this gaff prompted. I knew there would be a few, but I hoped they would see the humour in the slip-up as did my newsroom colleagues.

Of course, it was not the first time something like this has happened on air and you can bet it will not be the last. I'm reminded of a delightful moment supplied by my former co-anchor Pamela Martin, when during an intro to a story on bone-marrow donation her words became a bit tangled, and she described someone who had made such a donation as a "boner donor." It's very difficult to stifle a guffaw in a situation like that, but I managed to hold on even when others on the staff let go. And Pamela, who hadn't realized her gaff, could not understand the uproar until we explained it to her. Then she, too, joined in.

During my radio days at CHML in Hamilton, Ontario, it was my duty as the evening-shift news announcer to leave behind a collection of news bulletins when I left at midnight. These would be read throughout the after-midnight hours by the on-duty disc jockey who at that time was a chap named Fred Napoli, a chum of mine and today one of the most sought-after commercial announcers in the business. At the end of that long evening shift I was not always too careful about syntax or, for that matter, correct grammar. I only wanted to go home so I just tried to make the scripts simple and readable for the non-news personality who had to read them. So it was that in my haste one night I mistakenly ran the words "the" and "people" together to make it "thepeople." Fred, who obviously cared more about music than news, hit the words—or rather the combination thereof—and let fly with "thee-op-oh-lee" not once but on several occasions during the night because these little news nuggets were recyclable. Sitting at home, I wondered what the hell he was talking about and how that non-word had found its way onto the air. We didn't figure it out until much later and decided that the only way we got away with it was tied to the fact that his all-night audience listened but didn't necessarily hear.

When it comes to the new and seemingly unpronounceable names that pop up from time to time, especially in the coverage of international news, I take comfort in the belief that, if I don't know the correct way to say the name of some foreign dignitary or outpost in Afghanistan or wherever, chances are my viewers don't know either and anything is fair game until I can confirm it otherwise. That's probably why you hear so many different versions of those names until all of us find some common pronunciation. I know it happened with the names of UN Secretary General Kofi Annan and with Benjamin Netanyahu who is currently the prime minister of Israel. I've even done it to the names of some of our own reporters. I murdered Ron Benze's name the first time I had to introduce one of his reports. I called him Benz, as in Mercedes' partner, without realizing Ron pronounces the "e" on the end of his name. I apologized, of course, just as I did when I stumbled all over Anna Gebauer's name one night. I should have taken a cue from another old radio friend who, when confronted with the name of then-Soviet Foreign Minister Aroutunian, transformed it into "Mr. Rootin' Tootin'." And I will always remember sitting in my living room in Vancouver one day, watching one of our news productions and suddenly being startled by the anchor's version of Wichita, Kansas. It came out "Whi-cheet'-a" (emphasis on the second syllable) because, she explained later, she'd never seen the name in print before.

I also have a collection of Tony-isms, if you would like to call them that. Throw the word "molybdenum" into a script and there's every chance I'll kick it to pieces. And I've often stumbled, I hate to admit, on the word "Canada." Just too many syllables, I guess. I've yet to tackle Mahmoud Ahmadinejad, the name of the controversial president of Iran, but I suspect it would amount to carnage, and I'm never sure whether or not I'm pronouncing the name of the Ayatollah Ali Khamenei correctly or, for that matter, the name of the former US National Security advisor whose name looks like the letters on an eye chart, Zbigniew Brzezinski. It's not as if you can just pick up the phone and ask these people how they pronounce their own names. Sometimes, however, news announcers will reach a consensus on pronunciation by simply listening to each other and, it seems, eventually agreeing on what's right or wrong.

Spelling is often a problem on our broadcast when it comes to those visual displays that denote a person's name and title or a couple of words to define the gist of the story. For example, if I'm talking about wildfires in the BC Interior, what we call a "graphic" pops up beside me on the screen with the words "forest fires" under it. Hard to go wrong on that spelling. But in another case something caught a viewer's eye and she was moved to write:

> Hello, Is there anything that can be done about the frequent misspellings on the air? Please check your spelling before broadcasting to viewers. The other night the caption for Robert Dziekanski's mother's interview was "perusing charges" rather than "pursuing."

Dziekanski, as you may recall, was the forty-year-old Polish immigrant who died at Vancouver International Airport in October 2007 after being tasered five times by members of the RCMP who were trying to restrain him. The incident became the subject of a major judicial investigation and in the end threw a dark shadow over the reputation of the Mounties. And you may notice that our viewer, in her complaint about spelling errors, managed to spell Dziekanski's name right. But she wasn't quite finished with us yet. Something had caught her attention in another story we aired that involved a person being sought by local police. So she added to her note:

> Last night there was a piece regarding a suspect or missing person who walks with "a pronounced lisp." Was it supposed to be "talks with a pronounced lisp" or "walks with a pronounced limp"? These mistakes do no favours for our children's literacy nor speakers of English as a second language.

Good for her!

To state the obvious—and it almost seems silly to say this—reading properly, applying emphasis on words where it is required, knitting together the sense of a sentence and its relevance to the topic, and merely being able to tell a story as well as being able to spell are the prerequisites of what we news anchors do. It reflects on our credibility to let those things slip, even when a writer has made a mistake or gremlins have captured the computer system and created havoc. Perhaps, as some people will argue, the root of the problem lies in the educational system, but that doesn't mean we can deny our own responsibility to be professionals at what we have chosen to do.

In the past few years I have become so frustrated by mangled grammar that I have tried to hint to some of my colleagues that we seemed to be ignoring all the rules. My primary tool was the distribution of a couple of books that could get us all back on track. One seemed to me to be particularly apropos. It was written by Thomas Parrish and titled *The Grouchy Grammarian*. The subtitle is *A how-not-to guide to the 47 most common mistakes in English by journalists, broadcasters and others who should know better.* Parrish invented a fictional friend, the "Grouchy Grammarian" of the title, to lay out in a lighthearted but sometimes stern manner some of the pitfalls of our language and how often, perhaps without intending to, we slip up.

Most copies of the books I handed out are probably tucked away in the darkest corners of desk drawers in the newsroom, never to be seen again, and so the problem persists. I have not given up, but I will not be spending any more of the company's money trying in vain to set things right. I hate to think what will happen in this regard in newsrooms of the future if they carry on as they do today. But I'll be watching and waiting. I'll be as grouchy as the author of the aforementioned book, and I won't hesitate to pick up my phone or write a terse "letter to the editor," just as our viewer did.

15

The Oscars, the Nellies, the Tonys and Mine

As much as I appreciate the sentiment attached to awards, I'm not a fan of nor have I ever actively sought them. However, I do have my share, and some that I deem special hang on the walls of my home office. Still others are tucked away in sagging old cardboard boxes in my garage, part of the flotsam and jetsam of my career.

But my first award was not connected to my achievements in broadcasting but to a fling at acting. I was no more than eighteen and working in Stratford radio at the time and had become connected—I can't remember how—to a local amateur theatrical group. We were a group of teenagers bound by Catholicism and some kind of belief that we could put together a troupe that could take the local entertainment scene by storm. It was a bit like Mickey

Rooney encouraging Judy Garland and his other movie pals by waving his arms in the air and shouting, "Hey, gang, let's put on a play!" A buxom, to say the least, young organizer and cheerleader named Connie Trafagander grabbed the assignment as director and doled out the roles the rest of us were to play. I was cast as the warden in a prison drama, a grey-haired but sympathetic character, and the play revolved around the agony of this warden deciding the fate of a prisoner who during his incarceration had become a reformed criminal but not a shoo-in for parole. (The hair colour that was achieved via a makeup stick made me look, I thought, like Desi Arnaz of the Lucille Ball television series but turned my hair into a rock-hard helmet.) The play had a brief and successful local run and won a local drama festival, and then by virtue of that recognition we were invited to an even bigger event in nearby London, Ontario. I didn't think I had done that well in the production but, according to the judges, I was the best supporting actor of the festival. No one was more astounded than I was, but I gratefully accepted the accolade and took home a small plaque. I later dismantled the award and used the engraved plate attached to it as a bookmark.

It was a long time between that moment and my next award. *TV Week*, a Vancouver publication designed to rival the internationally known *TV Guide* and put out by my old friend Peter Legge, decided to establish an award program for local talent and the programs they fronted. The first awards night was a black-tie event that rivalled Oscar night in Hollywood, at least in our minds, and featured Bob Hope who was a friend of a friend of Peter Legge. It made for an impressive evening. For the next two or three years the *News Hour* scooped everything on the agenda, with BCTV staff making multiple trips to the podium and the devoted readers of *TV Week* repeatedly voting me the "Most Popular Anchor." When the constant winning became an embarrassment even to the recipients, it was finally decided that it didn't make sense to carry on decorating the walls of the homes of BCTV employees, and the awards were discontinued.

And then there was the President's Award for contributions to television journalism given to me by the Radio and Television News Directors Association in 1996. On that occasion I was flattered though slightly embarrassed, mostly for the association, that they handed me a commemorative plaque engraved with the year 1995. The mistake was actually pointed out by the president of the RTNDA, my friend Hudson Mack, who was at that time news director and anchor over at CHEK-TV in Victoria. He promised to redo the plaque with the appropriate year but it never happened.

After I was recognized as the "Italian-Canadian of 2002" by members of a couple of Vancouver Italo-Canadian business groups, I spent a considerable amount of time explaining to people, who knew nothing of my heritage, how the award came to be. One suggested that I might have been the only local celebrity in town and available that night and that probably the following year I'd show up to accept the "Asian-Canadian of the Year," if there was such a thing. Still, I knew that my mother would have been proud.

Also in 2002 I received notification that I would be one

of the Canadian recipients of the Queen's Jubilee Award. I had been nominated for the honour by retired senator Ray Perrault and I duly thanked him the next time we met. (Ray died in November 2008.) But some of the shine came off the honour a bit later. I guess I had expected to be invited to Ottawa or even perhaps to some plush anteroom in Buckingham Palace to meet her majesty, kneel, and accept the hardware. Imagine how disappointed I was when one morning among the bills and circulars in my mailbox was a large brown, very official-looking envelope. Inside was my award and the flashy medal hanging on the thick swatch of colourful silk that went with it. I was disappointed and pleased all at the same time. Some time later, after I had made a joking reference to my mailed-out medal, a special presentation was organized with Senator Ed Lawson presenting me with the framed medal and proclamation at a charity golf tournament for the BC Rehab Foundation.

Every once in a while I look up at it on my home office wall and smile as I think about my mother and her royalist leanings and how honoured on my behalf she might have been, despite the method of delivery. Perhaps it would even have made up for the time in March 1983 when I was invited to meet the Queen and the Duke of Edinburgh aboard the royal yacht *Britannia*, which was berthed in Vancouver during their visit. I turned down the chance to rub elbows with their royal highnesses on that occasion, and both my mother and my wife, who happened to be my mother's royalist equal, were not amused by my passing up the opportunity.

An award even more important to me was what most of

us in the Vancouver journalism family consider the ultimate recognition. In 2004 I was chosen to receive the prestigious "Lifetime Achievement Award" given annually in memory of that newspaper industry giant, Bruce Hutchison. Among his other achievements, he had served as the editor of the *Victoria Times* from 1950 to 1963 followed by sixteen years as editor of the *Vancouver Sun*. He was also the author of three books of fiction and twelve of non-fiction, including *The Unknown Country*, which won the Governor General's Award for Non-Fiction in 1943. He died at age 91 in 1992 after six decades as an outstanding BC-based journalist. It is thus very fitting that the Jack Webster Foundation should name its annual award in his honour.

Before I was chosen to receive it in October 2004, it had gone to thirteen media personalities including news-papermen Allan Fotheringham of the *Vancouver Sun* (and later the *Globe and Mail* and *MacLean's*), Denny Boyd of the *Vancouver Sun* and Jim Hume of the *Victoria Colonist*; political cartoonists Roy Peterson and Len Norris; radio personality Rafe Mair; and my old cohorts Cam Bell and Keith Bradbury. Although, to me, the very name of the award suggests an end to one's career as if there is nothing else to achieve, it's still one that I cherish, but on the night of recognition I was only able to blurt out a few thank-yous and to suggest that the honour would look good on my CV.

I have other bits and pieces given me for "just showing up," as it were, as a volunteer for various charitable organizations in the province, such as the annual Variety Club Telethon, which has been running for forty-three years and raising millions of dollars during that time for the care of stricken children in BC; the yearly fundraiser for BC Children's Hospital; and the Crossroads Hospice Society, which is dear to my heart simply because my involvement coincided with the death of my mother in 1994. I grieved alone but I came to know later that the society existed to give solace and understanding to people whose lives are suddenly thrown into turmoil by loss. Joining Crossroads gave me a chance to speak to their work and help raise money for a now-renowned facility, a hospice that caters to terminally-ill cancer victims and members of their grieving families. I continue to be deeply impressed by the dedication of the people who head the group and their devoted volunteers. They are selfless when it comes to making it all work and they make a huge contribution to our society as advocates for the dying. (And, by the way, their executive director, Barb Henhem, makes the best cookies in the world.)

My trophy wall also includes the previously mentioned honorary degree in technology granted to me in 2008 by the British Columbia Institute of Technology. (This was the award ceremony in which my dog, Jack the scene-stealer, figured so prominently.) It was, alas, a totally unearned award. I had served for a time on the Broadcast Journalism Advisory Board, a group made up of faculty members and selected broadcasters from around the province. My contribution was next to nothing and my tenure short-lived because I became less than enthusiastic about the BCIT program after I became convinced that, especially in the case of its night-school classes, it was accepting students based on their ability to pay rather than their ability to become broadcasters. It doesn't take a genius to pick the good seeds out of the chaff, and I thought that the faculty was not doing a very good job of it. I didn't make an issue of it, but I quietly backed away from my advisor role, content to invite some of the teachers and selected students to tour our studios and watch the *News Hour* as part of their ongoing education. I also went to speak to a couple of classes about career directions and the like, but that was as much as I gave of myself. Certainly nothing that warranted the honour of a doctorate. By the by, I can't use the title "Doctor" anywhere but on the BCIT campus. But Dr. Parsons just doesn't sound quite right anyway.

16

The Future of Broadcasting

IT'S BEEN SUGGESTED that given my fifty-plus years in the broadcasting industry, I must have seen it all. That may be true, but it's what's ahead for us that concerns me more. These are rough and unpredictable times for the television business. The winds of change are blowing at gale force, and it's hard to say who the survivors will be and who will ride out of the hills and shoot the wounded and emerge stronger and unscathed. But while the economic downturn of the late 2000s will surely take its toll, even before that there were signs that our industry was in for irrevocable changes. Certainly the pie had been cut into too many thin slices in the name of giving consumers access to the so-called five-hundred-channel universe. Consequently, conventional television came under siege because some companies had acquired more properties than they could financially handle in the long term.

In the Vancouver market the turmoil and jockeying for position began with the death of Frank Griffiths in 1994. Within four years his family had negotiated a deal to sell Western International Communications (WIC) to Shaw Communications Inc and CanWest Global Communications Corporation, subject to approval by the CRTC. Another two years of negotiations passed before the CRTC announced that it would approve CanWest Global's purchase of WIC Television, which included CHAN-TV (BCTV) and CHEK-TV (Victoria), but that approval was conditional on the purchaser divesting itself of CKVU-TV Vancouver, which CanWest had bought in 1988. These changes in ownership resulted in an unprecedented network shuffle in the Vancouver market: by September 2001 CKVU-TV had become an independent CHUM station, and CHAN-TV (BCTV) and CHEK-TV had become part of the Global Network. As a result, CHAN-TV was no longer available as a CTV affiliate, and that network transferred its affiliation to Baton Broadcasting's CIVT-TV. At the same time, the battle between cable TV operators and network owners was already taking on epic proportions. Who will win is unsure, but their scramble for a financial lifeline is breeding controversy and contempt in the boardrooms of Canada.

Back in 1957 when I first took my place in a radio studio in Stratford, Ontario, television was in its beginning stages in Canada. Radio, on the other hand, was still in its heyday, and anyone with a radio broadcasting licence in a small town or big was piling up advertising revenue, believing that the situation would never end. Those licences had truly become licences to make money. And, as an aside, I can tell you radio was fun in those days. It was less sophisticated than it later became, and a lot of us were merely making it up as we went along. Local radio personalities, mostly DJs, were stars in their communities, drawing moderate salaries, working a few hours a day for six days a week but thoroughly enjoying their involvement in what was then a very stable business. Creativity was encouraged, individuality expected, and broadcasting was better off for it.

But as television emerged from its period of growing pains and began to find its way into more and more homes, advertisers began to divert their dollars to a medium that had the added lure of pictures as well as sound. As those advertisers' revenues increased, so did their faith in television advertising, and radio began to feel a slight but perceptible pinch. In those first burgeoning years of the television industry I think we merely shrugged whenever another licence was issued in another part of the province or country because there was room for anyone with deep pockets and the ability to successfully convince the BBG, now the CRTC, that such-and-such a locale, even in the hinterlands, had a need for its own TV outlet. And helped by an affiliation with one of the networks and the competence of a fire-in-the-belly sales staff, most of these outlets survived. At the time, people like me could be added to the staff for praise and a few more pennies. We were all looking for a step-up and a way to crack the big time in the big town, so our struggles in the backwaters of the industry were tempered by the idea that some day we'd make it. News then was of the "rip-and-read" genre, and we were the talking heads who handled short programs with little in the way of production values until competition forced us to pick up our game. The leaders in the game came to understand that the broadcasting industry is technology-driven, that equipment is constantly being rendered obsolete by new inventions and innovations. Woe betide the station that falls behind in the technology department; today stations that want to keep up with the rest of the world respond to the changes and bite the financial bullet.

This technical side of the business is definitely not part of my expertise, but when I was in radio it was always gratifying to be presented with a new, improved tape recorder or later in television with a new camera that made my job easier and the product a bit more presentable. Back in the days of film it was not unusual to have my day's work rendered useless by scratches on the negatives or the absence of sound as I sat in a screening room or editing booth, awestruck by the destruction of my story. Time in the form of daily deadlines made any recovery at that point out of the question. It was soul-destroying, especially when I had to explain to the news director or the subject of that day's story that I had missed the six o'clock broadcast because I had been done-in by faulty equipment. And it happened too frequently. Stories just disappeared into the ether in a cloud of frustration and regret. The advent of videotape was a blessing. It allowed us reporters almost total control over our work inasmuch as it gave us the capability of screening our interviews or the pictures that enhanced our stories before we left the scene. If there were problems, we could easily reshoot, check it again, and if all was well, head for the newsroom knowing we could make a contribution that night at six. Life as a reporter became a whole lot easier.

Another of the innovations that caught everyone's eye and imagination was a gimmick called chroma-key that rendered the camera lens insensitive to the colours blue and green. It made it possible to project pictures onto the blue or green screen that popped up behind the anchor so that he appeared to be a presence in the scene during his introduction to the story. It was vastly overused, and the constant zooming must have made the average viewer quite dizzy, but the novelty, to producers and directors, was worth showing off again and again. It's still used today only in a much more sparing way. For example, Wayne Cox, our weather presenter, uses a green screen to display his maps and point out the pressure systems.

When I first began delivering the news on TV, we used the "stare and share system," meaning we shared our glances between the camera and the written script in front of us, not trying for a moment to convince the people in their living rooms that we were anything but "readers" wearing smart suits and colourful ties. Then to make the newscast more convincing and less distractive, we decided that we and the folks at home would be better served by technology—and that's where the teleprompter came in. I'm not a Luddite by any means, but I don't embrace technology with anything approaching fervour, so I argued against teleprompting devices on the basis that they made the newscast seem "artificial." Needless to say, I lost the argument and was soon staring at a script in the camera lens. This first device was awkward compared to today's computer-generated system. It consisted of a conveyor belt with a camera mounted over one end, the lens focussed on pages of script taped together in sequence as the pages came out of the typewriter stations around the newsroom. The camera would then transmit the image to the on-air camera in the nearby news studio. Occasionally pages were stuck together in the wrong order, and sometimes the script would suddenly bunch up and the newscaster would be literally lost for words because there simply weren't any. Or for some reason the belt would stop dead in its tracks. Fortunately, the anchor also had a copy of the script on the desk, but often I would forget to discard those pages that had already passed under the teleprompter camera, and when the belt stopped, I could be seen shuffling like mad to find my place.

However, there was one technological advance that was even harder for me to accept because it translated into the loss of jobs and, consequently, the loss of the friends and company on the studio floor who had always been a good gauge of how things were going. They had chided me good naturedly when I slipped up here and there, struggling with words, and never hesitated to give their own take on what was unfolding news-wise. Sadly the day came when they were all replaced by robots, cameras remotely controlled by one person who works a joystick and punches a computer board in a neighbouring control booth. Eleven people were displaced by the process. To the company's credit, they were moved into other jobs or offered financial packages in lieu of employment, but for me it was like losing family and it took me a long time to adjust.

I was so chary of the robots that I asked to preview them in an environment where they were already in use. As it happened, the same system was currently sliding around the studio floor at NBC's national news operation in New York City, the home base for Tom Brokaw, so I asked to be sent there to talk to Tom about the way he handled these new beasts. BCTV agreed to let me go, as much to placate me as anything, I think. To be honest, in the back of my mind was the prospect of an all-expenses-paid weekend trip and the chance to meet someone who my peers and I have held in high esteem for years. And that's the way it turned out. I took my then wife with me and asked my contract negotiator/financial advisor, Paul Shaw, to come along—at his own expense, of course. We arrived on a Friday, went straight to NBC studios for a tour of the facilities including the *Saturday Night Live* stage and then to a brief meeting with Brokaw. He was preparing for that night's show so he had little time to reassure me that "there-there" everything will be okay, now go away and let me get on with things. It all took about five minutes. My most enduring memories of the whole trip were his overpowering height (to me anyone over five foot eight is overpowering) and a trip to Tiffany's, which was much more important in the scheme of things as far as my wife was concerned than my worries about a looming battle with robots back home.

As it turned out, it wasn't much of a fight. Most operations with the same equipment leave the anchor to direct himself by reacting to the cues transmitted to his earpiece by someone in the control room. As a sop to my misgivings about the new system, BCTV allowed me to have a floor director, a terrific guy named Bryan Small, who physically points me in the right direction, lets me know how much time is left in a current report and cues me to start the next item in the show—babysitting me, so to speak, through the presentation. And he's now been with me for twenty years as the guardian of my comfort zone. What pampered animals news anchors are!

It is true, of course, that the age we're living in is more about technology than anything else. I recently spent some time in California playing golf with a few pals, one of whom carried along his new iPhone. Not on the course, mind you. That's simply not allowed. But everywhere else, whenever he had the chance, he demonstrated the benefits of this cutting edge, must-have, handful of technological excellence. It's hard to imagine so much stuffed into so little space— e-mail, a GPS system to take you almost anywhere, list upon list of phone numbers, addresses and birthday dates, Facebook, YouTube, Twitter, stock market quotes, weather forecasts, highway traffic conditions, favourite television commercials, pictures of your family, and on and on. It was totally wasted on me. I couldn't even begin to program the contraption and if I did, chances are I'd lose it all in the single press of the wrong combination of buttons and would have to start all over again. The computer on which I wrote this book is used for only one purpose—writing—and for that, so far so good.

I'm not a total technology dunce. In my skinny arsenal of gadgetry I have something called a Kindle. It's an electronic book or, perhaps more accurately, an electronic library. I purchased it in the US through Amazon, the online bookstore. With this and a credit card, I can tap into a list of thousands of publications, newspapers and magazines and download whatever appeals to me, read it at my leisure, keep it forever, have hundreds of titles to choose from but only have one book-sized device to cart around. The only problem is that although it has been available for several years in the US, at the time of writing it was still not officially available in Canada. Amazon suggested this was the fault of Canadian publishers, but since almost none of the books on Kindle are Canadian-published, that excuse does not hold water. I thought of my Kindle when I came across a cartoon in my morning paper recently. It depicted the stately building that houses the main public library in New York with a sign fronting it that reads "Museum of the Internet" and beneath that a note that reads "formerly the New York Public Library."

I think, perhaps, that my point here is that, as far as television stations are concerned, if you live by technology, you could just as easily die by technology. For the station owner the cost of new equipment erodes the bottom line, and simply keeping up with technology is a fool's game because, as soon as you go to a high-definition system, someone will surely perfect three-dimensional transmissions and here we go again. On the other hand, investing in new technology is probably money well spent, even if keeping up with competitors is a costly proposition and explaining the process to board members and shareholders is a daunting task indeed. In the past it was even more so if the owner believed, as one station executive once told me, that "news programming is a loss leader." I can only presume that his comment was a red herring to keep me and others from trying to negotiate better salaries or benefits when it came time for contract renewals. The cost of talent was significantly higher then than it is now as company managers and financial officers are being advised to pare expenses in areas where costs might be considered out of control. After I joined BCTV in 1974 to anchor the *News Hour,* my salary climbed rapidly over a series of agreements to enviable heights that even I sometimes found breathtaking. Never the level reached by network anchors in the US system, but certainly high by Canadian broadcasting standards. I was told, in fact, that at one time I was the highest salaried local anchor in the country. I doubt very much that pay packets throughout the ranks in TV newsrooms will be as fat and flattering a few years from now as they once were.

As a journalist, I could only applaud back in the '70s when BCTV decided to put more of its eggs into the news basket. News director Cameron Bell and his second-in-command, Keith Bradbury, with the urging of their boss, Ray Peters, went full throttle to create a morning news offering, then an hour-long package at noon, followed at five by another half-hour of news and at six by the *News Hour*, the flagship program that attracted so many viewers. Finally, to end the day they inserted another forty-five-minute show at eleven thirty to follow—in the days when the station was a

CTV affiliate—the *National News* with the venerable Lloyd Robertson at the helm. To my recollection no other station in the country dedicated so much in the way of resources, money included, to delivering that amount of information on a daily basis. Later we introduced Saturday and Sunday news programming in the morning, at noon and in the evening to complement our Monday through Friday efforts.

In 1993 because it was felt that Canadians needed an earlier hit of national news, we introduced *Canada Tonight* for the half-hour from five thirty to six. However, right from the start I knew that the show would be a tough sell simply because it couldn't sustain itself on a shoestring budget and a story mix that included a lot of features, leftovers from anywhere we could find them, but very little hard news. We could always call on our Ottawa bureau to come up with coverage of the day's events on Parliament Hill or pressure another station in the network to supply a timely piece here and there, but we had no reporters dedicated to our program in other important outposts. Thus, *Canada Tonight* became a ratings failure and a shadow of what I hoped it might have been. Only pride kept it going as long as it did, but when Global TV became our parent company in 2001, it died a quiet death to be replaced by Global's national news with Kevin Newman.

Many of us at Global Network stations resented the creation of a national news program inasmuch as it put more pressure on local newsrooms to become contributors to the program while at the same time taking big bites out of our own resources. In an interview with BC's *TV Week* I openly criticized the move, pointing out that several of our better reporters had been seconded to the national show without regard, in our case especially, to the maintenance of a highly successful local program. I referred particularly to Tara Nelson, a terrific reporter with an easy on-camera persona, who went on to become Global's bureau chief in London, England. I could see why they had poached her, but that wasn't my point. While it might have been seen as a dog-in-the-manger approach on my part and I certainly didn't want to stand in the way of any who wanted to advance their careers, it stuck in my craw to be treated as a sort of a "farm team."

The day after that interview was published I found myself sitting in the office of our station manager, Roy Gardner, after I'd been slapped on the wrist by news director Ian Haysom for other remarks I'd made about what I considered to be the lack of solid content in the *News Hour*. Our assignment editor, Clive Jackson, took wild exception to my criticism since content was his bailiwick, and Haysom had no choice but to take me to task. I stuck to my guns. Clive, for whom I have a lasting admiration, eventually cooled off and our friendship survived, but there was no noticeable change at six o'clock. For his part, Gardner was disturbed that I had gone public with my complaint, but I sensed that he didn't totally disagree with my stand. He had over the years been a strong *News Hour* defender and knew its importance, along with the other news programs in our lineup, in the general well-being of BCTV, or as it had become when he called me onto the carpet, Global TV in BC.

The years with Western International Communications

(WIC) had been happy and satisfying for all of us at BCTV, and we had relished our success and the backing of our management team who always made sure we had the wherewithal to do the job. The Griffiths family, who owned WIC, had other broadcasting interests, including the highly successful radio operation CKNW in Vancouver. However, WIC had none of the crushing debt that Global had taken on over the years that followed Izzy Asper's deal with Conrad Black to purchase his fourteen major dailies, including the *Vancouver Sun* and the *Province*, along with a clutch of eighteen other papers and a 50 percent share in the *National Post*. In the preceding years CanWest, the Asper company that had acquired the Global TV Network back in the late 1980s, had also piled up interest in broadcast outlets in New Zealand, Australia and even Chile. As a result, part of our dismay at being acquired by Global might have been our fear of becoming a much smaller entity in the scheme of things, whereas before we had been a major player in the WIC group. I know that we certainly wondered how long it would be, given CanWest Global's debt circumstances, before the taps on the money pipeline between Vancouver and our new head office in Winnipeg would be squeezed shut.

We watched our new bosses carve out space in our already crowded newsroom to make room for Global National's base of operations and second certain members of our reporting staff to the new endeavour. At the time, however, Global was intent on proving that not every significant national newscast had to be based in Toronto. Of course, we wondered about the extent of that commitment when the brass gave in to a request to have the on-air segment of the show moved to the national capital. In the beginning we shared the technical components needed to air our individual news programs, though the problems created by that process led to a certain amount of resentment between the two factions. After awhile we began to co-exist, learned to share what we could, even applauded each other's victories and commiserated on our shortcomings. None of this would have taken place without the professional input of the local Vancouver operation and the ability to swallow hard and carry on when Global began to spend more money on its national production, opening up reporting stations and bureaus in selected parts of the world. Even though we were living through budget struggles at our level, we gave in to the theory that, without its own national newscast, Global could not really claim to be a network. When the recession landed on the world at large in 2008, conventional television took a body blow. As the economy nose-dived, so did advertising revenues. It's hard to sell a thirty- or sixty-second commercial to someone whose business is on the downturn, and even the toughest, most imaginative sales force would be hard pressed to convince clients that self-promotion is the road to economic salvation. That complication, together with a debt load created by acquisition put our network and other broadcasting entities into a deep funk. Banks and other lenders and impatient investors want and expect financial returns for their backing despite the obvious plight of our industry.

When the networks began brainstorming over their predicament, among their first responses was a move to divest themselves of the burden of those stations that simply, even in relatively good times, were not turning a profit. For Global that meant stations in Victoria, Kelowna and Hamilton, another in Quebec and one situated in Alberta. They were the member stations in Global's so-called secondary network, dubbed "E!," which turned out to be more of a drain on the corporate purse than it was worth and was therefore expendable. Their sale, if it ever happened, would go toward reducing the billions of dollars of debt accumulated over the years. However, I doubt very much if the return on such a sale, even if a buyer could be found in such tough times, would put much of a dent in the huge amount owing to creditors.

CTV, which also has huge media holdings, including the *Globe and Mail* newspaper, took a similar route, offering up a handful of its struggling TV stations to the highest bidder or any other "reasonable offer." Oddly enough, as if to rub their noses in it, Shaw Cable offered CTV a dollar for each of the three stations on the block, and the offer was accepted. Then a little later Shaw withdrew the offer and retreated. Go figure. The third player, the CBC or Mother Corporation, has kept going by cutting staff, something the other two nets had already done in their major markets. And there were programming cuts for all three as well.

Besides fighting for survival as conventional broadcasters, CTV and Global, together with the Quebec-based TVA group owned by Quebecor, recently had to fight another battle over renewal of their licences. A hearing before the CRTC in Gatineau, Quebec, pitted them against cable operators across the country over "fee for carriage."

What the broadcasters want is a share of the revenue realized by cable companies and satellite providers who charge their subscribers, as part of a monthly fee, for receiving signals from, say, Global BC or CFTO in Toronto. Currently specialty channels such as TSN and HGTV do get such revenue from the cable and satellite operators and enjoy as well whatever they can earn from advertising. Even though Global, CTV and TVA have financial interests in certain specialty channels, they feel they should have a secondary source of income for distribution of their conventional signals. They argue that their operations are much more costly than programming a specialty channel and that they are subject to much greater losses when the revenue stream fed by advertising begins to dry up. To this end, CTV launched an appeal to its viewers to back their demands for a carriage fee with a "Save Local TV" campaign, and CanWest, with its back against a financial wall, tried to explain to its employees, investors and creditors that a decision in its favour would go a long way toward helping ease the pressure on its bank balance.

For its part, Shaw, using its considerable clout as a cable giant, tried a pre-emptive strike outside the hearing room. Over the signature of its bold leader, Jim Shaw, it advertised in the pages of daily newspapers across the country, many of them, of course, owned by CanWest. In an attention-getting, full-page blue and white newspaper ad, Shaw attacked the three national networks, CTV, Global and CBC, for going with a begging bowl to millions of households, cable and satellite customers, asking for what amounted to "a direct tax." Shaw argued that the conventional broadcasters were asking Canadians to fix their problems while at the same time spending billions of dollars "acquiring foreign programming, TV stations and newspapers" and "starving local programming across the country for years." The ad accused CTV in particular of buying US programming only to leave it off their prime-time lineups, effectively keeping it away from their competitors, while ignoring the need for more local programming in their schedules. It accused all three of its opponents of threatening to cut local newscasts and jobs and to close television stations, which they had already signalled they would do if sent away by the Commission without the requested "bailout." (It was about this time that Shaw enhanced its "white knight" image by offering to purchase the stations CTV had promised to jettison.) The message to consumers argued that the three nets were holding viewers hostage with the ransom being a six-dollar monthly increase on their cable bills, while providing no assurances that more money would go into local programs or new jobs. Shaw attempted to convince Canadians that the big three broadcasters were asking to be rewarded for their poor performance, shirking their duty and ignoring the requirements of their licences, and all this after being turned down twice before in similar appearances before the CRTC. "These companies," the ad went on, "need to be accountable for their decisions. They should spend less time misleading Canadians and more time managing their business and producing local programming." Summing up, the ad proclaimed:

Canadian broadcasting faces an exciting future. The government has done a remarkable job kick-starting the economy, creating jobs, eliminating unnecessary taxes and assisting Canadian television production. A new tax would drag this progress down. If broadcasters get this bailout, you can be sure they will be back for more.

In front of the federal broadcast watchdog, CTV argued that the "old ways" simply do not work anymore, that Shaw and Rogers were raking in the dollars from multiple sources of income while conventional operations had only what they could make from the proceeds of advertising. In addition, CTV and the other networks were asking for an increase in industry-wide contributions to the Local Programming Improvement Fund—a fund established to underwrite the expense of local programming—from the current 1 percent to 3 percent. At the same time the networks stopped short of suggesting that more money, if it was forthcoming, would be put to more local programming across the country. In fact, CTV Network's CEO, Ivan Fecan, when asked about use of the extra revenue replied, "We would have what we currently have. It would continue."

And so the arguments continued much, we suspect, to the frustration of Konrad von Finckenstein, the head of the CRTC. After the combatants had their say in Gatineau, he appeared before a parliamentary committee investigating the status of the Canadian broadcasting industry and seemed to throw up his hands in surrender by suggesting that cable distributors and over-the-air broadcasters get together and determine their own payment plan. He told committee members, "They're putting on a very good show. They need each other. They [meaning CanWest and CTV] have a stable of specialty channels, and for each one of those they negotiate a fee. Why can't they do that for their conventional stations? They know each other and they know each other's businesses and markets." Perhaps it will come to that, but, as of this writing, the fight rages on. You can't help but wonder, though, if the average viewer, unless he is required to put out more money every month, really gives a damn. How many times have you wondered as you watched your favourite show, Canadian or American, where it came from or how it got from there into your living room? Not often, I suspect.

The two things that have continually fluctuated in this business over the past couple of decades, especially when it comes to the dissemination of news, are content and presentation. Take note of these observations by Howard Kurtz, who fronts a media criticism program on CNN. In his book, *Reality Show: Inside the Last Great Television News War*, he writes, "The newscasts have an aging audience because they constantly cater to that audience, squeezing out, or simply ignoring, all kinds of cool developments that might appeal to younger people. That is a ticking demographic time bomb." It is Kurtz's opinion that the three American networks are not unlike the Detroit automakers "churning out a product that fewer customers want even as they equip the latest models with shinier chrome and bigger tail fins." Of course, that scene is changing as the carmakers regroup under the pressure of recession and with the help of government bailouts and they begin retooling for a thinned-out product line.

But the comparison may not be far off the mark. For so long broadcasters, believing that only they and certain focus groups know what the consumer wants, have been filling evening newscasts with feature reports on health care issues, environmental concerns and other lifestyle considerations, compressing the time allowed for the real news of the day. The excuse might be made in the case of local news programming that we have to provide enough content to fit into a sixty-minute span rather than the networks' thirty minutes and that, therefore, a certain amount of chaff will find its way onto the air. But it must be galling for producers to have to pull legitimate news stories to make way for these other reports that might be sheer bulk and less informative than they claim to be, aimed at a limited segment of the audience.

Others will argue that, faced with a two-hour run of news between five and seven in the evening as we have on Global BC, the real juggling act is trying to avoid repetition, and because a story has been covered earlier, when it comes around to six o'clock, that story is expendable. This argument assumes, of course, that the channel has the same audience in its grip for two hours and that viewers won't find what they need at some other source. It's not as if the Internet doesn't exist and that Yahoo and Google don't provide news, or that coverage isn't available on specialty channels like CNN, CTV News, MSNBC and Fox that deliver nothing but news. And don't we, so often, direct viewers to the web for "more details," photos, extended versions of interviews, other opinions or sidebars? In fact, a nightly part of our broadcast on Global TV in BC is the instruction to our viewers that "For more on this story, go to our website at www-dot" etc. It is almost as if we are now giving away what we have been asking our advertisers to help us pay for.

There is also little doubt that advertising on the Internet will add another complication to the life of the broadcasting industry, and it will have an impact on our newspaper cousins as well because they are having their own struggle with a changing world. I have no inside information on their plight, but like so many observers I wonder why the *Vancouver Sun* ran a week-long series of articles that seemed as much an exercise designed to convince themselves as well as their readers that the daily newspaper as we know it is not an endangered species. This came amid reports that some papers in major markets across the country were suffering from circulation problems while others, such as the *National Post*, were cutting publication by one day a week. In the US it is much more dire. The *Sun-Times* of Chicago filed for bankruptcy in March 2009 as did the parent companies of dailies in Los Angeles, Philadelphia and Minneapolis. Two other notable publications have had financial daggers plunged into their hearts. After 150 years of publishing, the venerable old *Rocky Mountain News*, the number-two paper in Denver, Colorado, succumbed in February 2009, as did the *Seattle Post Intelligencer*, the second paper in the Seattle market, one month later.

However, the *Vancouver Sun*, in its series on newspaper survival, argued that the US market had to cope with higher production costs and operated under a different business model than its Canadian counterparts and that, when the economic downturn swept across this country, the effect had nowhere near the severity of the situation in the US. Advertisers, said the *Sun*, were not abandoning papers here but were simply becoming more deliberate about the way they buy newspaper space, for instance, picking fewer products to promote and concentrating more on getting a reasonable return on an advertising investment.

Dennis Skulsky, president and CEO of CanWest Publishing, saw it this way:

> There will be newspapers. The business model in Canada in particular is certainly still viable but that doesn't mean it is viable forever. We have to continue to evolve and we have to get leaner. We have to invest in the future and hire and bring people into the business that move easily among the media platforms today in a digital generation.

Skulsky outlined his version of the future as one where newspapers deliver a print-based version of a newspaper to one home in a neighbourhood, a digital version to a user on a personal computer in the home next door and yet another electronic version to a third neighbour on his iPhone or other handheld device. And according to my computer, these options are already on the way. I am a subscriber to both the *Vancouver Sun* and the *Province*, and my laptop reminds me every morning via e-mail that I can at no extra cost plug into the *Sun*'s online version of its daily edition.

If I have already read the copy delivered to my door and done the daily crossword puzzle why, I ask myself, would I want to do that? And conversely why would I bother with paper if technology via the Internet gives me all the information I require? If two papers don't do it, what more can the digital copy provide? And, while I think of it, why do I subscribe to two newspapers that deal in essentially the same information—except perhaps on the editorial pages or when one of these papers scores an exclusive story as the result of dogged investigative reporting—in a market that also offers a free newspaper that I can simply pluck from a box a block from my house? I think the tactile aspect of newspapers has something to do with their viability. I guess you could call it news you can feel. Or could it be a choice of format—the broadsheet *Sun* versus the tabloid-style *Province*—that keeps the two alive and competitive? In Toronto, as I recall, the *Sun* newspaper was popular because its size was more amenable to a good morning read on the subway, and the same applies in London, England, where tabloid-style papers like the *Daily Mirror* and the *Evening Standard* are the papers of choice among users of the underground.

In the meantime the future of television news remains a matter of widespread discussion. No one seems to have a grasp on what will emerge at the end of the next five to ten years, given what's going on today. The question of how to satisfy the fiscal needs of broadcasters and consumers at the same time gives rise to a lot of speculation and head-scratching. Cable operators probably will be happy with the status quo and will continue to plump up the goose that fills the nest with golden eggs, while conventional broad-casters will probably find themselves making their way in a very different world.

Here, however, is the way I see it. News program-ming attracts a big share of advertising, so unless stations find another way to duplicate that revenue, don't expect wholesale change. On the other hand, news is expensive programming, so station operators have created a dilemma that might only be resolved by reducing the number of hours dedicated to daily information. Should breakfast television necessarily take up four to five hours a morning even in the name of Canadian content? Or should we cut it back? Should we look at a half-hour of news, weather and sports during the lunch hour, relieving the pressure on resources while providing a quick fix for news junkies who want a traditional serving of news before going back to the Internet? Will we get over the idea that we have to be all things to all people, still providing a service to afternoon-drive commuters and the exhausted business people who arrive home, heavy with briefcase, but ready for their daily dose of information during the so-called supper hour? After all, these have been our "traditional" viewers for years. And then should we be revving everything up again to send other people off to bed thinking they now know everything they need to know and their world is safe?

I doubt that in the long term there will be a need for on-air television stations to provide so much informational programming when faced with the total accessibility of the Internet. That's not to say that the CNNs and MSNBCs as well as the CTV Newsnets of the world will not be around to send out quick summaries of information, and it is easy to see that they could function well as providers of late-breaking stories and updated material, weather and sports details for a generation that needs to be comforted by the presence on the screen of someone like myself. People still find that reassuring now, but will a new audience that is redefining its options care after the next decade when hopefully the confusion in the marketplace has been sorted out? The point is: do we need multiple sources of television news, the dozen or so channels devoted to sports coverage, the radio frequency that delivers only traffic information or the duplication of newspaper-style news coverage in the large market areas across the country? Will less eventually be more? I really hope the changes that must be made will not just spawn more "reality shows," the cheap, down-and-dirty, most often embarrassing offerings that have become the vogue in the past few years. I know they have an audience, but frankly they make me shudder. (Of course, maybe that style of show based on life in a typical Canadian newsroom would provide a two-in-one answer for all manner of tastes in our vast audience!)

Finally, here's an observation from Shachi Kurl, a young broadcast journalist who, though fairly new to the business, is gathering experience as the legislative reporter for the A-Channel in Victoria. Her point of reference was in a column carried by the *Vancouver Sun* on the death of music icon Michael Jackson. The day he died—and I watched this as well—she couldn't help but notice that the confirmation of the singer's death came, not from the three major American networks or CNN, but from TMZ, Thirty

Mile Zone, a website with its own regular TV show but considered by the big three nets and CNN to be an upstart in the news game, merely a purveyor of celebrity and entertainment information. But while the others hemmed and hawed over "official notification" of Jackson's passing, TMZ boldly delivered the confirmation that he was indeed dead, and left the others in the journalistic dust. All of which led Shachi to write:

> I never worked in TV when the news side was far better paid thanks to the crazy money pulled in through must-see shows. Remember when CBC had *Dallas*. Remember when people actually sat down and watched *The Andy Griffith Show* on CTV plus the commercials in between. I graduated from J-school just as newspapers were moving en masse to free online content, and not long before YouTube and free downloads made it seemingly unnecessary to watch anything on TV. The situation is hardly tenable for us hacks. The fact is news is business. Business must make money or it will die. Money is made by selling a product people want to pay for. And if infotainment, in all its hedonistic, vacuous glory, is making money for my employer, then who am I to complain? TMZ may just save my career. I shouldn't be blaming Michael Jackson. I should be thanking him.

As Shachi wrote her piece new developments in the broadcasting business were flying all around us. Rather than resolve the dispute between cable operators and broad-casters with over-the-air operations, the CRTC decided to try to bring about a détente by firing the "fee for carriage" issue back at the disputants, challenging them to resolve it on their own by determining a compensation plan that would satisfy the demands of the conventional broadcast-ers. Barring any agreement, the CRTC would then arbi-trate a deal. At the same time the federal regulators tried to cushion the effect of the 2009 economic crisis on local television stations across the country by embellishing its Local Programming Improvement Fund. It decided that cable and satellite providers should chip in more money to help fund news and other local programming for sta-tions with less than a million viewers. This was too late, I'm afraid, for at least one station in the Global chain. At about the same time the CRTC was handing out this new largesse, Global was calling together staff members at CHEK-TV in Victoria during their lunch hour to tell them that within weeks they would all be looking for other jobs. CHEK would not survive the financial struggle that put it and operations in Hamilton and Kelowna on the block.

CHCH in Hamilton was eventually acquired for a fire-sale price by Channel Zero, a Montreal operator that also bought the Global station the network had offered in Zero's home city. Viewers of Kelowna's CHBC were reassured of having their local station when Global decided it was worth keeping after all and reinstated it as an affiliate of the regular Global Network, admitting that the E! brand—E for entertainment—had not worked. It's worth mentioning that the Victoria market will still have a local outlet, the

A-Channel station, so the argument that Vancouver Island would be without its own station carried less weight than the voices of protest in Kelowna that said without CHBC the city would lose its local voice. Look for more changes in British Columbia's broadcast landscape as time moves on and circumstances inevitably change.

17

Uncle Walter et al.

As I struggled to meet the deadline for the publication of this book, Walter Cronkite died. Had he survived a few more months he would have marked his ninety-sixth birthday, and his passing brought a flood of well-deserved tributes. He was, after all, a legend in our business, perhaps *the* legend. He had become as much a part of journalistic history as the events he described on the CBS *Nightly News* from the first year he took over that broadcast in the early sixties to the day when he reluctantly took mandatory retirement in March 1981.

If you have lived through the Cronkite era and especially during his ascension to his status as the "most trusted man in America," you will have sat on the edge of the living room couch as he described, with tears welling in his eyes, the death of President John F. Kennedy on that dark and fateful day in Dallas, Texas. On that November day in

1963 I was working as a reporter for CHML Radio news in Hamilton and had been assigned to cover a court case in Burlington, Ontario. It was an hour or so after lunch and I was in a phone booth near the courthouse reporting details of my story to an editor in the newsroom, and just as I began dictating the judge's decision, I was told to "hold the line" because of a breaking news story. But rather than put me on hold, the editor laid the phone on his desk, and that is how I heard what had transpired in Texas as the presidential motorcade had manoeuvred past the soon-to-be-famous Texas Book Depository where Lee Harvey Oswald lay in wait, a high-powered rifle cradled on a windowsill with the crosshairs of its scope fixed on the approaching presidential limousine. As I listened to the developing chaos in our newsroom, I knew that my story had been rendered insignificant. It would not make that night's broadcast. There was nothing to talk about but those tragic moments in Dallas, and most people would have flipped on their TV sets to watch and listen to Cronkite's telling of the terrible event.

In earlier years you would have watched, deeply enthralled, as Cronkite shuddered with excitement as he described the Apollo Mission astronauts' landing on the moon. In preparation for the lunar touchdown, he had versed himself in everything there was to know at that time about space exploration and rocketry, and that knowledge showed, despite some seemingly untoward but playful comments, as he drew us into the drama. Unable to contain his excitement, he urged Apollo to "Go, baby, go!" as it lifted off the launch pad, and he threw out the unseemly words "hot diggety dog!" as the huge module fired its jets to begin its journey back to earth. But, no matter, he became the "go-to" anchor throughout all the important subsequent missions, the Apollo and Gemini series, launched by NASA from Cape Kennedy, more widely known now as Cape Canaveral, in Florida.

By now everyone must know the famous story of Cronkite's "involvement" in the war in Vietnam. Despite Washington's assurances, it became his assessment that the controversial conflict would not produce a clear winner, and when he offered up this observation, President Lyndon Johnson was moved to say, "If I've lost Cronkite, I've lost middle-America." Such was the respect Cronkite commanded from the average American "man on the street" as well as the "man in the White House," that American involvement in Vietnam subsequently began to dwindle. It would be wrong, in my opinion, to suggest that Walter Cronkite used his position or his status for any manner of personal gain or influence. I prefer to think that he attained his position through a mix of dedication and circumstance tied to his sense of what was intrinsically right for America and what was wrong. However, his own version of his place in the world was contained in an interview with the *Christian Science Monitor* in 1973, in which he said, "I am a news presenter, a news broadcaster, an anchorman, a managing editor, not a commentator or analyst. I feel no compulsion to be a pundit."

Writer Doug James, in his 1991 biography of Cronkite wrote that "his approach was not so much a cold and disembodied television network news reader as a caring and concerned Victorian father who gathered his family around him in the parlor after dinner to read the newspaper aloud and explain the day's events." Most of us who follow in Walter's awesome footsteps wish, I'm sure, that we could impart that kind of image on a nightly basis at six.

I never aspired to be an anchor. At first I was happy doing a daily DJ shift in southern Ontario. When it became apparent that I couldn't sustain the charade, that I couldn't bend my personality to make it appear what it wasn't, I looked about the radio station in Hamilton, Ontario, and decided that I would be better suited to a quieter existence as a news writer. And that's how my career began. Since then, through some fortunate manoeuvring and happenstance, I am where I am, having had—so far—what I consider a successful career. I say "so far" because, even though I am in my seventy-first year, full retirement is not even a consideration. As one Monty Python character is often quoted as saying; "I'm not dead yet."

I have written earlier how my first experience as an anchor was, to say the least, a knee-knocking affair. Had it not been for the kindly words of Annis Stukus, I'm sure I would never have made it through that first night. But that was only the first hurdle in my television career. The next came one night just a few years later. Moments before my appearance in front of the cameras with a research piece I had prepared, the biggest butterflies on the planet swooped down on me, and a panic attack took over. When Joe Mariash, the anchor at the time, threw the broadcast to me for my piece, my mouth opened but no words came out. Instead, I gasped for breath. It was only a dozen seconds, though it seemed like an agony of minutes, before I could recover enough to throw it back to Joe, almost begging him to carry on while I tried to catch my breath. I never made it back on air that night. Later in a bit of a puff piece in *TV Guide* on my emerging career, the writer described it as an unfortunate "breathing spasm" and said that I had handled it well. As the incident was soon forgotten by others, I must have thought I'd gotten away with something and I carried on.

But stage fright jumped up and bit me several more times over the years. After I was hired to front the *News Hour* on BCTV, a similar thing happened, only this time it was more prolonged. This was back in the days when I had the time and inclination to rehearse, and as I sat at the anchor desk going over my script, fear reached out and grabbed me. I seized up. It was apparent to me that, even as I opened my mouth to say, "Good Evening," the going would be tough. I found it helped when I put my hand to my mouth and coughed then apologized. But all through that show and many others for a long period of time afterward, the same problem occurred. I became unravelled and I even contemplated giving it all up. Luckily, I figured a way out. I realized that just in those last moments before the *News Hour* went to air I needed some kind of mental diversion, some way to get my mind off what was ahead and how frightened I had become. So I turned to Shakespeare. Literally. One of my favourite Shakespeare quotations comes from *King Richard II:*

> This royal throne of kings, this scepter'd isle,
> This earth of majesty, this seat of Mars,

> This other Eden, demi-paradise,
> This fortress built by Nature for herself
> Against infection and the hand of war.
> This happy breed of men, this little world,
> This precious stone set in the silver sea,
> Which serves it in the office of a wall,
> Or as a moat defensive to a house,
> Against the envy of less happier lands,
> This blessed plot, this earth, this realm, this England.

I thought that if I concentrated on those words just before I was to say, "Good Evening," it would disconnect me from the hour-long dread I was facing. And it worked. I would bend over the pages of my script as if I was reviewing the content, but I would be silently whispering to myself those words by the Bard. In time, these feelings of dread—and they are very hard to understand or to describe—dissipated and I faced the nightly broadcast with a lot more confidence and a lot less trepidation. Thanks, Mr. Shakespeare!

It used to frustrate me when, after describing what I have done for a living all these years, some people would respond with a comment about a huge salary and a short work day. And I was amused by Jonathan Elias's description of anchors in general when he, as a reporter, encountered them in the newsrooms where he landed his first jobs. He had joined the ranks of TV news reporters in the mid-1980s and described the so-called on-air talent he worked with in the western US in those days as "glorified meat-puppets, blow-dried know-nothings who rolled in just before their newscast, read through their scripts and delivered the news without so much as setting a wingtip on the mean streets of the market." I was tempted to say, "Yo, Jonathan, get a grip!" But since he passed that judgment, Elias has become an anchor himself at WBZ in Boston, one of the largest markets below the border, and he has acquired a load of awards, among them a batch of Emmys and a prestigious Peabody, which he shares with other reporters at a station in Minnesota.

And you know what? Elias was right about those anchors. That used to be the case in a lot of markets where anchors were gods and revered, even by station owners and network executives, as the "franchise." I readily admit to receiving special treatment at times as an anchor, though in Canada we don't share the same lofty stage as our American counterparts. I never actively sought any favours but some certainly came my way because of my profile as a newsman. But Elias shares in a shrinking legacy because ironically he anchors the evening newscasts at a station that in earlier times could well afford to pay outrageous salaries to those "princes of anchordom." Back in the early sixties, however, when I applied to WBZ Boston for a reporter-anchor job, I didn't think that the salary they were offering was acceptable and I skulked back to Toronto. Otherwise, I could have been a "meat-puppet," too.

Increasingly these days, anchors are being forced to combine their presenting skills with their reporting abilities. Salaries are going down as management struggles through a recession that has seen reduced advertising revenues in markets that have become steadily more competitive. The landscape, as they say, is rapidly changing. Jeff Alan saw it coming back in 2003 when he wrote his book, *Anchoring America: the Changing Face of Network News.* He surveyed the lives and contributions of nineteen men and women in this news business, from Walter Cronkite to Connie Chung, whom he considered to have been, as he put it, "admired, reviled, criticized, threatened, lauded, hated, loved and emulated by different sections of the public, but never ignored." Having done that, he concluded that:

> Whatever the shape of news to come, anchors continue to prove their value because they are storytellers. And the storytelling device draws in just as it did in the days of Homer and Herodotus. The anchors are presenters, but essentially they are storytellers and bards who traffic in fact rather than fiction. Their study and mastery of storytelling devices, cadence, tone and personal style will allow them to survive not only the evening news broadcasts but the very networks that gave life to anchoring.

Alan, like a lot of us, had not reckoned on a recession and the changes it wrought, but I suppose he offers hope if you are an anchor in these trying, troubling times. But I consider myself a part-time anchor now. Others describe it as semi-retirement. As I look back, I revel in my success, but there has always been a lingering doubt in my mind. As I confided to a friend during a trip to Las Vegas a few years ago, I've always had a feeling that sometime, somewhere, someone would tap me on the shoulder and say, "Uh-h, sorry, Mr. Parsons, but we really had someone else in mind when we gave you your career and your success, and now we must ask you to give back everything you've received."

No way.

Icc 1/10
SO 3/10
OK 7/10
TAP 10/10
GCC 2/11
Tapi 2/11
OK 9/12
CG 7/15
SGP 6/16
SO 10/16
VGH 6/17